The
Four Great
Pillars in the
Lord's Recovery

Witness Lee

The Holy Word for Morning Revival

Living Stream Ministry
Anaheim, CA • www.lsm.org

First Edition, October 2011.

ISBN 978-0-7363-4924-6

Published by

Living Stream Ministry
2431 W. La Palma Ave., Anaheim, CA 92801 U.S.A.
P. O. Box 2121, Anaheim, CA 92814 U.S.A.

Printed in the United States of America

11 12 13 14 15 / 7 6 5 4 3 2 1

Contents

iv

Preface

1. This book is intended as an aid to believers in developing a daily time of morning revival with the Lord in His word. At the same time, it provides a limited review of the International Training for Elders and Responsible Ones on "The Four Great Pillars in the Lord's Recovery" held in Baarlo, Netherlands, October 6-8, 2011. Through intimate contact with the Lord in His word, the believers can be constituted with life and truth and thereby equipped to prophesy in the meetings of the church unto the building up of the Body of Christ.

2. The entire content of this book is taken from the published training outlines, the text and footnotes of the Recovery Version of the Bible, selections from the writings of Witness Lee and Watchman Nee, and *Hymns,* all of which are published by Living Stream Ministry.

3. The book is divided into weeks. One training message is covered per week. Each week presents first the message outline, followed by six daily portions, a hymn, and then some space for writing. The message outline has been divided into days, corresponding to the six daily portions. Each daily portion covers certain points and begins with a section entitled "Morning Nourishment." This section contains selected verses and a short reading that can provide rich spiritual nourishment through intimate fellowship with the Lord. The "Morning Nourishment" is followed by a section entitled "Today's Reading," a longer portion of ministry related to the day's main points. Each day's portion concludes with a short list of references for further reading and some space for the saints to make notes concerning their spiritual inspiration, enlightenment, and enjoyment to serve as a reminder of what they have received of the Lord that day.

4. The space provided at the end of each week is for composing a short prophecy. This prophecy can be composed by considering all of our daily notes, the "harvest" of our inspirations during the week, and preparing a main point

with some sub-points to be spoken in the church meetings for the organic building up of the Body of Christ.

5. Following the last week in this volume, we have provided reading schedules for both the Old and New Testaments in the Recovery Version with footnotes. These schedules are arranged so that one can read through both the Old and New Testaments of the Recovery Version with footnotes in two years.

6. As a practical aid to the saints' feeding on the Word throughout the day, we have provided verse cards at the end of the volume, which correspond to each day's scripture reading. These may be removed and carried along as a source of spiritual enlightenment and nourishment in the saints' daily lives.

7. The training message outlines were compiled by Living Stream Ministry from the writings of Witness Lee and Watchman Nee. The outlines, footnotes, and references in the Recovery Version of the Bible are by Witness Lee. All of the other references cited in this publication are from the published ministry of Witness Lee and Watchman Nee.

International Training
for Elders and Responsible Ones
(Fall 2011)

General Subject:

The Four Great Pillars
in the Lord's Recovery

Truth, Life, the Church, and the Gospel

Scripture Reading: John 18:37; 11:25; 14:6; 1 Tim. 3:15-16; Eph. 1:13; Col. 1:5

Day 1

I. **The Lord's recovery is mainly founded upon four pillars: truth, life, the church, and the gospel (Eph. 1:13; 4:18; 5:23-25, 29, 32; 6:15).**

II. **The first great pillar in the Lord's recovery is the truth (John 18:37):**

A. The Lord's recovery is the recovery of the divine truths as revealed in the Word of God (2 Tim. 3:16).

B. The Lord's word, His truth, is in the Bible, but the Bible needs the proper interpretation (2:15).

C. The truth is absolute in itself, and we must be absolute for the truth (2 John 1-2, 4; 3 John 3-4, 7-8).

D. The standard of the Lord's recovery depends upon the standard of the truth we put out; the truths will be the measure and the standard (John 18:37).

Day 2

E. The kind of church we build up depends on the kind of truth we teach; thus, there is a desperate need of the living truth to produce the church, to help the church to exist, and to build up the church (1 Tim. 3:15).

F. We need to have the truth wrought into us and constituted into our being (1 John 1:8; 2:4; 2 John 1-2; 3 John 3-4):

1. To be constituted with the truth is to have the intrinsic element of the divine revelation wrought into us to become our constituent, our intrinsic being, our organic constitution (John 17:17).

2. The solid truth that is constituted into us becomes in us a constant and long-term nourishment (1 Tim. 2:4; 2 Thes. 2:13).

G. If the truth is wrought into us and constituted into our being, we will be able to protect the interests of the riches of God's divinity and the attainments of His consummation (Rev. 21:12a, 17).

Day 3   **III. The second great pillar in the Lord's recovery is life (John 14:6; 11:25):**

A. Both the truth and the life are the Lord Himself, but they are two different aspects of what He is (14:6):

1. The truth is the outward definition and explanation, and life is the inward and intrinsic content (8:32; 11:25).

2. The Lord is in us as our life, but the experience of life needs an explanation; this explanation is the truth (Col. 3:4; 1:5):

a. If we receive the Lord according to this explanation, we have life; in order to experience and enjoy the Lord as life, we must know the truth (1 John 1:1-2, 5-6).

b. The experience of the Lord as life is contained in the Lord as the truth (John 14:6).

3. If we are not clear about the truth and do not understand or know the truth, we will have no way to enjoy the Lord as our life (8:32; 11:25).

B. The Lord wants His church to know Him as the truth and to receive and enjoy Him as life, and the content of the church must be the growth of Christ in us as truth and life (Matt. 16:18; 1 Tim. 2:4; John 8:32; 10:10).

C. Life is the Triune God dispensed into us and living in us—God the Father as the source of life, God the Son as the embodiment of life, and God the Spirit as the flow of life (Rom. 8:2, 10, 6, 11; John 5:26; 1:4; 1 John 5:11-12; Rev. 22:1).

D. Life is the way to fulfill God's purpose; God's desire for man to express Him in His image and to rule in Him with His dominion can be realized only by God's life (Gen. 1:26; 2:9).

Day 4   **IV. The third great pillar in the Lord's recovery is the church (1 Tim. 3:15-16):**

A. The Lord's recovery is a recovery of the truth and of life so that He may have the church; the truth brings in life, and once we have life, we become the church (John 18:37; 10:10; 1 Cor. 10:32).

B. The church is the house of the living God (1 Tim. 3:15):
  1. As the house of God, the church is the dwelling place of God—the place where God can have His rest and put His trust (Eph. 2:21-22).
  2. The church as the house of God is the Father's house, the enlarged, universal, divine-human incorporation (John 14:2; 12:23; 13:31-32).
C. The church is the supporting pillar and the holding base of the truth (1 Tim. 3:15):
  1. *Truth* in 1 Timothy 3:15 refers to the real things revealed in the New Testament concerning Christ and the church (Matt. 16:16, 18; Eph. 5:32).
  2. As the pillar, which bears the truth, and the base, which holds the pillar, the church testifies the truth, the reality, of Christ as the mystery of God and of the church as the mystery of Christ (Col. 2:2; Eph. 3:4).

Day 5

D. The church is the corporate manifestation of God in the flesh (1 Tim. 3:15-16):
  1. God's manifestation was first in Christ as an individual expression in the flesh (v. 16; Col. 2:9; John 1:1, 14).
  2. God is manifested in the church as His enlarged, corporate expression in the flesh (Eph. 2:19; 1:22-23).
  3. The great mystery of godliness is that God has become man so that man may become God in life and nature but not in the Godhead to produce a corporate God-man for the manifestation of God in the flesh (Rom. 8:3; 1:3-4; Eph. 4:24).

V. **The fourth great pillar in the Lord's recovery is the gospel (1:13; Col. 1:5):**
  A. The gospel that we preach in the Lord's recovery is the purest, highest, most complete gospel (Rom. 1:1, 3-4; Mark 1:14-15; Acts 20:24; Eph. 3:8; 6:15; 2 Cor. 4:4).

B. The gospel includes all the truths in the Bible; the entire Bible is the gospel of God (Eph. 1:13; Col. 1:5):

1. The truth is the gospel, and the light of the truth is the light of the gospel (Mark 1:1, 14-15; John 8:12, 32).

2. We should not think that the gospel is one thing and that the truth is another thing (Eph. 1:13):

   a. The truth is the gospel, and our preaching of the truth is the preaching of the gospel (Col. 1:5).

   b. To preach the gospel is actually to speak the truth, because the real gospel preaching is the speaking of the truth (Acts 8:4, 12, 30-35).

3. For the preaching of the high gospel, we have a strong burden to encourage everyone to pursue the knowledge of the truth (1 Tim. 2:4):

   a. We should study the truth to the extent that we can expound the truth and announce the truth; this is to preach the high gospel.

   b. If we are filled with the truth inwardly, we will spontaneously express it outwardly by speaking the mystery of the gospel to people (1 Thes. 1:8; Eph. 6:19).

4. The commission of the church today is to preach the gospel, the content of which is the truth; our preaching of the truth is the preaching of the high gospel (Mark 16:15; 1 Tim. 2:4).

Morning Nourishment

2 Tim. Be diligent to present yourself approved to God, an
2:15   unashamed workman, cutting straight the word of
        the truth.
3:16   All Scripture is God-breathed and profitable for teach-
        ing, for conviction, for correction, for instruction in
        righteousness.

The Lord's recovery is mainly founded upon four pillars: the
truth, life, the church, and the gospel. The reason Christianity is
degraded is that it has lost the truth and is short of life. The Bible
tells us that the Lord Himself is the truth and the life. In John
14:6 the Lord Jesus said, "I am the way and the reality and the
life." In this verse the reality is the truth. Thus, the Lord said that
He Himself is the life and the truth. (*Truth, Life, the Church, and
the Gospel—the Four Great Pillars in the Lord's Recovery*, p. 69)

Today's Reading

First, the Lord's recovery is the recovery of the divine truths as
revealed in the holy Scriptures, the holy Word of God (2 Tim.
3:16). The divine truths are not according to what anyone thinks
or imagines; they are revealed in the...[Bible]. The Bible is a great
blessing that God, the Lord, has given to mankind on this earth. If
there had not been such a book as the Bible...on the earth, what a
pity and what a devastation there would have been among the
human race! The Bible is justifiably called "the Book" because the
Bible is "the Book" among all books. The Bible is the book of books
because it is in this book that we can see all the divine truths.
(*1993 Blending Conference Messages concerning the Lord's Recovery and Our Present Need*, p. 13)

Today we need Ezras to teach the people, to educate them, and
to constitute them with the heavenly truths....In Ephesians 3:8
Paul speaks not only of Christ's riches but of Christ's unsearchable
riches. Today the enjoyment of the riches of Christ is by His word.

In His recovery the Lord is moving by His word, by the truth.
His word is in the Bible, but the Bible needs the proper interpretation. (*Life-study of Ezra*, pp. 34-35)

There is the need of the word of the truth, rightly unfolded, to enlighten the darkened people, inoculate against the poison, swallow up the death, and bring the distracted back to the proper track. (2 Tim. 2:15, footnote 2)

In learning to take care of God's work, one basic lesson is to be absolute for the truth. No truth in the Bible should be entangled with man's condition....When man entangles the truth with his own condition, he feels that he cannot speak the truth if he has not experienced it. Yet we have to realize that it is not our experience which qualifies us to speak concerning a truth. Truth is absolute in itself. David said that all men speak vanity (Psa. 12:2). When he spoke this word, he was not considering himself. Before God, David considered himself as nonexistent. God's servants cannot look inward into themselves. God's truth is absolute; it is not involved with us in any way. Because the truth is absolute, we have to sacrifice ourselves and put ourselves aside.

We have to realize that the condition of an individual has nothing to do with God's truth. If truth is affected by man, the truth is no longer the truth. If the truth is not something absolute for you, you do not know God, and you do not know God's word. (*The Collected Works of Watchman Nee,* vol. 57, pp. 135-136)

Today we are here for the Lord's recovery. For the long run, we surely have to help the saints in the Lord's recovery to get into the top spiritual education. You must remember that we still uplift the living Christ, the life-giving Spirit, life itself and its riches, and the church in a living way. To promote these things, to carry these things out, and to bring people into these things so that they remain there, we need the Word and we need the truth. The standard of the Lord's recovery depends upon the standard of the truth we put out. The truths will be the measure and the standard. (*Elders' Training, Book 3: The Way to Carry Out the Vision,* p. 102)

Further Reading: Truth, Life, the Church, and the Gospel—the Four Great Pillars in the Lord's Recovery, chs. 1, 3-4; The Collected Works of Watchman Nee, vol. 57, pp. 135-138

Enlightenment and inspiration: _____

_____

_____

_____

Morning Nourishment

John   ...For this I have been born, and for this I have come
18:37 into the world, that I would testify to the truth. Every-
       one who is of the truth hears My voice.

3 John For I rejoiced greatly at the brothers' coming and tes-
3-4   tifying to your *steadfastness in the* truth, even as you
       walk in truth. I have no greater joy than these things,
       that I hear that my children are walking in the truth.

What kind of church you will build up depends upon what kind of truth you teach....If we had not had a Bible in our hands during the past 2,000 years since the Lord Jesus resurrected and ascended to the heavens, everything would be in the air and nothing could be solid. Even the things concerning the Spirit could not be solid. The Spirit depends upon the Word. This is why the Lord said that the words that He spoke to us are spirit (John 6:63). The words which the Lord speaks are the solid spirit. Without the Word the Spirit is not so solid. Without the Word the Spirit might be just "a phantom." Today, however, we have the Bible. (*Elders' Training, Book 3: The Way to Carry Out the Vision*, p. 100)

Today's Reading

We have seen that whenever people contact the holy Word, many times they get the Spirit, but it is hard to give an instance where people touch the Spirit and then they get the Word....This is history. A principle has been set up through history that there is the desperate need of the living truth to produce the church, to help the church exist, and to build up the church.

We must do our best to get ourselves into these truths and to get these truths constituted into our being. This cannot be done within a short time, but this must be our practice. I also am burdened that all the leading ones, either the elders or the serving ones taking some kind of lead, should have a real burden to pray for the saints in your locality that the Lord may stir up their interest, their seeking heart, and their spirit to seek after the Lord in His truth. The truth is nowhere but in the Bible, yet the Bible needs an opener. We need to lead the saints into the real, right, and proper realization of the need of the Bible.

I believe that we all have to admit that a good number of saints have been meeting with us year after year, yet if you check with them today, you would discover that not much intrinsic element of the divine revelation has been really wrought and constituted into their being. Not only in the matter of life but even more in the matter of the truth not much intrinsic element has been wrought into the saints. I am really concerned that not many among us can present particular truths in an adequate way.

When what we read becomes a truth in our being, this nourishment remains forever. What I have received is not all the time inspiration, like a vapor. What I have received from the Lord is always the solid truth, so it remains in me, nourishing me all the time. You must have the truth. The only way for the truth to get into you is through your mentality. Then it remains in your memory. If you do not understand, the truth cannot get into you. The truth gets into you through your mentality, your understanding. Also, if the truth gets into your memory, it becomes a constant and long-term nourishment. Then you have an accumulation of the truth, and you are a person continually under the constant nourishment. You will then know how to present the truth to others, not merely to inspire them or to stir them up, but to make them solid and constituted with the truth. (*Elders' Training, Book 3: The Way to Carry Out the Vision*, pp. 100, 105, 88, 93)

[One] function of the wall of the holy city with its foundations is to protect the interest of the riches of God's divinity on the earth and the attainments of His consummation....[However], those who do not see the riches of the Father's divinity do not know how to protect them....We must put out the pure truth from the Word to protect the interest of the riches of God's divinity. (*The Application of the Interpretation of the New Jerusalem to the Seeking Believers*, pp. 32-33)

Further Reading: Elders' Training, Book 3: The Way to Carry Out the Vision, chs. 9-10

Enlightenment and inspiration: _____

_____

_____

_____

Morning Nourishment

John **Jesus said to him, I am the way and the reality and the**
14:6 **life; no one comes to the Father except through Me.**
Rom. **And if the Spirit of the One who raised Jesus from the**
8:11 **dead dwells in you, He who raised Christ from the**
dead will also give life to your mortal bodies through
His Spirit who indwells you.

Both the truth and the life are the Lord Himself, but they are
two different aspects of what He is. The difference is that the truth
is an outward definition and explanation, and life is the inward
and intrinsic content. The Lord is in us as our life, but the experience of life needs an explanation. This explanation is the truth. If
we receive the Lord according to this explanation, we have life.
Hence, in order to experience and enjoy the Lord as life, we must
know the truth. The experience of the Lord as life is contained in
the Lord as the truth. If we are not clear about the truth and do
not understand or know the truth, we will have no way to enjoy
the Lord as our life. For this reason we must spend an adequate
amount of time to learn the truth. (*Truth, Life, the Church, and
the Gospel—the Four Great Pillars in the Lord's Recovery*, p. 69)

Today's Reading

The Lord has not left us in darkness. Today all of His truths
are contained in the Bible, which He has given to us. We must
realize that the Bible is a book of life. The reason the Bible is a
book of life is that its entire content is truth. All experienced
Christians confess that no one can enjoy Christ as life if he does not
know the Bible or understand the truth in the Bible. We need to
go to the supermarkets to buy food for our physical body to be fed
and sustained. In like manner, we must come to the Bible to receive
the truth that is in it if we want to receive and enjoy the Lord as
life. All the truths in the Bible are food for our spiritual life.

The Bible is not merely a book of knowledge. All the knowledge contained in the Bible is in fact truth, and in this truth, life is
concealed. When we read the Bible, if we study only the letter but
not the intrinsic truth within, we will not receive life. Hence,

every Bible reader has to see the truth that is conveyed through the letter of the Word. Once we see the truth, we will spontaneously touch life.

Today the Lord's recovery is a recovery of the truth and of life. We all know that the decline of Christianity is due to the fact that it has lost both the truth and life. This loss of the truth and life eventually produced many human methods and worldly organizations, which are not what the Lord wants. The Lord does not want any organization or human method. Instead, He wants His church to know Him as the truth and to receive and enjoy Him as life. The entire content of the church must be the growth of Christ in us as truth and life....In the churches we do not want to have any organization or human methods. Rather, we want to minister to God's people for their growth by planting and watering as the apostle Paul said in 1 Corinthians 3:6 and 9. (*Truth, Life, the Church, and the Gospel—the Four Great Pillars in the Lord's Recovery,* pp. 69-71)

The Son is the embodiment of the Father, and the Spirit is the reality of the Son....Life is the Triune God dispensed into us and living in us. The Father is the source, the Son is the course, and the Spirit is the flow. The Triune God is dispensed into us in His Divine Trinity and is now living within us. (*Basic Lessons on Life,* pp. 58-59)

We have seen that God's desire is for man to be filled with His life that man might express Him in His image and rule in Him with His dominion. God's desire for man to express Him and for man to have dominion over His enemy can be realized only by God's life. Thus, we see in Genesis 2 that God placed man in front of the tree of life with the intention that man would take God as life into himself (vv. 8-9). Genesis 2 also says that a river went out of Eden to water the garden (v. 10), showing that when we partake of God as life, we are brought into the fellowship, the flow, of this life. (*The Crucial Revelation of Life in the Scriptures,* p. 17)

Further Reading: Truth, Life, the Church, and the Gospel—the Four Great Pillars in the Lord's Recovery, chs. 5-6

Enlightenment and inspiration: _____

_____

_____

_____

Morning Nourishment

**1 Tim. But if I delay, *I write* that you may know how one
3:15-16 ought to conduct himself in the house of God, which
is the church of the living God, the pillar and base of
the truth. And confessedly, great is the mystery of
godliness: He who was manifested in the flesh, justified in the Spirit, seen by angels, preached among the
nations, believed on in the world, taken up in glory.**

The four pillars in the Lord's recovery are the truth, life, the
church, and the gospel. In the New Testament the first person
is Christ and the second person is the church....The church was
produced by Christ, Christ is the Head of the church, and the
church is the Body of Christ. A human body is not an organization but a living organism. Likewise, the church is not an organization but an organism. As believers, we are the members of
this organism. (*Truth, Life, the Church, and the Gospel—the Four
Great Pillars in the Lord's Recovery*, p. 105)

Today's Reading

First Timothy 3:15b says, "The church...the pillar and base of
the truth." This indicates that without the truth, there would be no
church. The truth brings in life, and once we have life, we become
the church. (*Truth, Life, the Church, and the Gospel—the Four Great
Pillars in the Lord's Recovery*, p. 127)

As the house of God, the church is the dwelling place of God.
Ephesians 2:22 says, "In whom you also are being built together
into a dwelling place of God in spirit."...Paul is saying that the
local saints, the saints in Ephesus, were being built together in
Christ into a dwelling place of God.

The church, the dwelling place of God on earth, is the place in
which God can have His rest and put His trust. In this dwelling
place God lives and moves to accomplish His will and satisfy the
desire of His heart.

Because the church is God's dwelling place, the church is
where God expresses Himself. A house is always the best place
for a person to express himself. The kind of person you are is

expressed by your house....The principle is the same with the church as the dwelling place of God. In His house, His dwelling place, God expresses Himself on earth. This is the reason 1 Timothy 3:16 reveals that the church is God's manifestation in the flesh. God not only desires to make home in the church and to have a resting place there; He also wants to express Himself in the church. He wants to practice His New Testament economy, speak forth His desire, and manifest His glory in the church. All that He is, all that He is doing, and all that He wants to obtain are to be manifested, expressed, in the church as His dwelling place.

The Triune God in eternity past held a council (Acts 2:23) to make a decision that the second among Them had to become a man and pass through the processes of human living, death, and resurrection so that all the redeemed and regenerated believers of God would be incorporated into God's incorporation to be an enlarged, divine-human incorporation. The processed and consummated Triune God and the redeemed and regenerated believers became an enlarged, universal, divine-human incorporation in the resurrection of Christ (John 14:20), consummating the New Jerusalem as the tabernacle of God (Rev. 21:2-3). (*The Conclusion of the New Testament,* pp. 2229, 4186)

The church of the living God is "the pillar and base of the truth" [1 Tim. 3:15]. The pillar supports the building, and the base holds the pillar. The church is such a supporting pillar and holding base of the truth. *Truth* refers to the real things revealed in the New Testament concerning Christ and the church....God's New Testament economy is composed of two mysteries: Christ as the mystery of God (Col. 2:2) and the church as the mystery of Christ (Eph. 3:4)....The church as the supporting pillar and holding base of the truth testifies the truth, the reality, of Christ as the mystery of God and the church as the mystery of Christ. (*Truth Lessons—Level Three,* vol. 4, pp. 57-58)

Further Reading: Truth, Life, the Church, and the Gospel—the Four Great Pillars in the Lord's Recovery, chs. 8-9

Enlightenment and inspiration: _____

_____
_____
_____

Morning Nourishment

Eph. And He subjected all things under His feet and gave
1:22-23 Him *to be* Head over all things to the church, which is
His Body, the fullness of the One who fills all in all.
6:15 And having shod your feet with the firm foundation
of the gospel of peace.

In the church life God should be manifested in the flesh. Even though we are in the flesh, we should not live by the flesh. We should live in and by resurrection so that God may live in our living, making us Him in His attributes as our virtues for His manifestation.

First Timothy 3:15-16 indicates that not only Christ Himself as the Head is the manifestation of God in the flesh but also that the church as the Body of Christ and the house of God is the manifestation of God in the flesh—the mystery of godliness. According to the context, *godliness* in verse 16 refers not only to piety but also to the living of God in the church, that is, to God as life lived out in the church. Both Christ and the church are the mystery of godliness, expressing God in the flesh. The church life is the expression of God; therefore, the mystery of godliness is the living of a proper church (1 Cor. 14:24-25). God is manifested in the church—the house of God and the Body of Christ—as His enlarged corporate expression in the flesh (Eph. 2:19; 1:22-23). (*The Conclusion of the New Testament,* p. 3664)

Today's Reading

The manifestation of God in the flesh began with Christ when He was on earth (John 14:9). The manifestation of God in the flesh continues with the church, which is the increase, enlargement, and multiplication of the manifestation of God in the flesh (1 Tim. 3:15-16). Such a church becomes the continuation of Christ's manifestation of God in the flesh—Christ lived out of the church as the manifestation of God. This is God manifested in the flesh in a wider way according to the New Testament principle of incarnation (1 Cor. 7:40; Gal. 2:20). The principle of incarnation is that God enters into man and mingles Himself with man to make man one with Himself (John 15:4-5). The principle of incarnation means that divinity is brought into humanity and works within humanity (1 Cor. 6:17; 7:40; 1 Tim. 4:1). The great mystery of godliness is that God has become man so that man may become God in life and nature but not in the Godhead to produce a corporate God-man for the manifestation of God in the flesh (Rom. 8:3; 1:3-4; Eph. 4:24).

Although we were sinners, we have been redeemed out of our sinful position and sinful situation. We are now redeemed ones. God has imparted Himself into us, making us one with Him and also making Him one with us. First Corinthians 6:17 says, "He who is joined to the Lord is one spirit." This is the great mystery of godliness—God manifested in the flesh. We are the same as God in the divine life, the divine nature, the divine element, and the divine essence but not in the Godhead. (*The Conclusion of the New Testament,* pp. 3664-3665)

In the last days of this age, the Lord has raised us up and given us a twofold commission: on the one hand, we are to dispose of everything negative, and on the other hand, we are to preach to people—not in part but in full—the pure, high, and complete gospel. This preaching is not done through inviting a spiritual giant to do the speaking; that is not according to the Bible. The Lord wants us to go.

Today our preaching of the gospel and the truth is not inviting people to our "restaurant" but delivering food to their homes. Not only do we need to know people's situation, but more importantly we need to preach to them the pure, high, and complete gospel. Then little by little we can teach them the pure, high, and complete truth. In this way the Lord will be able to gain a proper church prepared as His bride so that He can come back to marry us. This is our commission today. (*The Mystery of the Universe and the Meaning of Human Life,* pp. 66-67)

Further Reading: The Conclusion of the New Testament, msg. 363;
  The Mystery of the Universe and the Meaning of Human Life,
  chs. 5-6

Enlightenment and inspiration: _____

_____

_____

_____

Morning Nourishment

1 Tim.   This is good and acceptable in the sight of our Savior
2:3-4   God, who desires all men to be saved and to come to
         the full knowledge of the truth.
Col.   Because of the hope laid up for you in the heavens, of
1:5   which you heard before in the word of the truth of the
         gospel.

The four pillars in the Lord's recovery are truth, life, the church, and the gospel. The truth brings us life, life produces the church, and the church is responsible for the preaching of the gospel.

The unique commission of the church today is to preach the gospel, the content of which is the truth. The truth tells us one central point: the Triune God—the Father, the Son, and the Spirit—is dispensing Himself into us—sinful, tripartite men—that our sins may be forgiven and that we may receive God's life and have God Himself in us for our transformation into the sons of God. This is the truth and the gospel. We must learn the truth.

Today the reason that the gospel of the Lord cannot be spread is that we do not know the truth. The truth is the gospel. If we speak the truth in every place, we are in fact preaching the gospel in every place. The entire Bible is the gospel of God, but it seems that we do not understand this. Now we have to turn this situation around so that all the saints among us will know how to speak the truth and preach the gospel. This will provide the Lord a broad way to fulfill His desire. (*Truth, Life, the Church, and the Gospel— the Four Great Pillars in the Lord's Recovery,* pp. 121, 127, 101)

Today's Reading

Do not think that the gospel is one thing and that the truth is another thing. The truth is the gospel, and our preaching of the truth is the preaching of the gospel. To preach the gospel is not to tell people about escaping perdition and going to heaven nor to tell them about prosperity and peace. It is to tell people about God, about Christ Jesus, and about the church. In other words, to preach the gospel is to tell people that God wants to enter into man and make sinners sons of God, that these sons of God are living members of Christ for the constitution of the church, and that these ones are in the church, which is expressed in different localities, so that they can live the church life in the local churches.

For the preaching of the high gospel, we have a strong burden to encourage everyone to pursue the knowledge of the truth....If we are filled with the truth inwardly, we will spontaneously express it outwardly by speaking the mystery of the gospel to people.

We all have the heart to preach the gospel, but if we do not know the truth, we will quickly run out of words as soon as we open our mouths to speak to people. After two or three sentences we will not know what to say. In the end, we will have nothing to say, and people will be unwilling to listen to us. Hence, we must learn the truth. The word of the gospel is the truth. For us to speak the word of the truth, we must first learn the truth. If from now on we would be willing to seriously learn the truth, we all would know how to preach the gospel in two months. To preach the gospel is actually to speak the truth, because the real gospel preaching is the speaking of the truth. To speak the truth is to preach the gospel; thus, we all must learn the truth in a proper way.

The result of society's civilization and progress has been an unremitting emptiness within man. Only the high truths in the Lord's recovery can fill up this emptiness. Therefore, we should bear this burden to diligently study the truth to the extent that we can expound the truth and announce the truth. This is to truly preach the gospel. This is the preaching of the high gospel. Paul said that God had commissioned him to preach the gospel and to teach the truth (1 Tim. 2:7). In the same way, this commission has been given to us today. I hope that we would all receive this commission to actively preach the gospel and teach the truth. (*Truth, Life, the Church, and the Gospel—the Four Great Pillars in the Lord's Recovery*, pp. 123, 125-126, 41)

Further Reading: Truth, Life, the Church, and the Gospel—the Four Great Pillars in the Lord's Recovery, ch. 10; *The Mystery of the Universe and the Meaning of Human Life*, ch. 7

Enlightenment and inspiration: _____

_____

_____

_____

Hymns, #819

1   As the body is the fulness
      To express our life,
    So to Christ the Church, His Body,
      Doth express His life.

2   E'en as Eve is part of Adam
      Taken out of him,
    So the Church is Christ's own increase
      With Himself within.

3   As from out the buried kernel
      Many grains are formed,
    As the grains together blended
      To a loaf are formed;

4   So the Church, of many Christians,
      Christ doth multiply,
    Him expressing as one Body,
      God to glorify.

5   As the branches of the grapevine
      Are its outward spread,
    With it one, abiding, bearing
      Clusters in its stead;

6   So the Church's many members
      Christ's enlargement are,
    One with Him in life and living,
      Spreading Him afar.

7   Fulness, increase, duplication,
      His expression full,
    Growth and spread, continuation,
      Surplus plentiful,

8   Is the Church to Christ, and thereby
      God in Christ may be
    Glorified thru His redeemed ones
      To eternity.

9   Thus the Church and Christ together,
      God's great mystery,
    Is the mingling of the Godhead
      With humanity.

Composition for prophecy with main point and sub-points: _____

_____

_____

_____

_____

_____

_____

_____

_____

_____

_____

_____

_____

_____

_____

_____

_____

_____

_____

_____

_____

_____

_____

_____

_____

_____

_____

_____

_____

_____

_____

_____

_____

_____

The First Great Pillar—Truth
(1)
Being Sanctified by the Truth
to Move out of Ourselves and
into the Triune God for the Oneness

Scripture Reading: John 17:14-24

I. **Truth is the divine light shining on the facts of the Bible and televising a heavenly, spiritual vision of these facts into our being:**
   A. In the New Testament, truth denotes this kind of "heavenly television."
   B. The Lord is the light, the truth, and the Word; the Word, which is also the truth, gives light, for in the Word there is light (John 8:12; 14:6; 17:17; Psa. 119:105).
   C. Truth is the shining of the light, the expression of the light; in other words, truth is light expressed.
   D. The Spirit is called the Spirit of truth, the Spirit of reality (John 14:17); the Spirit of reality is the "heavenly electricity" by which spiritual things are televised into our being.
   E. When the Spirit of truth, the Spirit of reality, shines upon the spiritual facts recorded and contained in the Bible, we receive the truth, reality.
   F. If we read the Word without the shining of the Spirit, we may have doctrine or "news reports" but not the truth, the reality, or the vision.
   G. All the divine facts are contained in the Word and conveyed to us through the Word; when the Spirit shines upon the Word, we have the "heavenly television"; the light shines upon the facts in the Word and conveys a heavenly vision of these facts into our being, and we know the truth (cf. Eph. 1:17-18a).

II. **There are two functions of the truth:**
   A. The truth sets us free from the bondage of sin, freeing us from all the negative things (John 8:32, 36).

B. The truth sanctifies us positionally and dispositionally, saturating us with the element of God (17:17; Eph. 5:26).

Day 3 III. **The Triune God in His Word realized by us and being imparted and infused into our being is the truth that sets us free and sanctifies us:**

A. When we are disappointed or depressed, feeling empty within, we can open ourselves and come to the Word; after reading for a while, something within us rises up, and we enjoy the presence of the Lord.

B. By taking the Word in this way, something of the Lord is wrought into us; this is the reality of the Triune God living, moving, working, and separating us.

C. Every morning we can touch the living Word and have the divine reality, the Triune God, infused into our being:

1. This transfusion of the element of God frees us from such negative things as temper, jealousy, hatred, and pride; it sets us free from every kind of falsehood, and we have real liberation, real freedom.

2. As we are being set free, we are also sanctified, separated, made holy to God, not only positionally but also dispositionally; we become one with God because His very essence is wrought into us.

D. Daily we need to come to the Word in this way; we need to come to the Word every morning and, if possible, at other times as well.

E. When the Word is mingled with the living Spirit in our spirit, we are sanctified with the essence of God.

F. By contacting the Word in this way, God is added into us day by day; as a result, we are permeated with God and made one with Him.

G. Our crucial need is to have the living Triune God infused and wrought into us through the written

Word, the living Word, and the applied word of God.

Day 4   **IV. Sanctification through the word of the truth results in oneness by dealing with the factors of division; truth sanctifies, and sanctification issues in oneness (John 17:14-24):**

A. The Lord Jesus, the Son, is the truth; the Spirit is the Spirit of truth; and the Father's word is the truth (1:14, 17; 14:6, 17; 17:17; 1 John 5:6):

    1. The Father is embodied in the Son, the Son is realized as the Spirit of truth, and the Spirit is one with the Word (John 6:63; Eph. 6:17).

    2. Whenever we come to the Word with an open heart and an open spirit, we immediately touch both the Word and the Spirit as the truth.

B. The sanctifying word, the sanctifying Spirit, the sanctifying life, and the sanctifying God are all one; therefore, if we are being sanctified, we are one spontaneously because all the factors of division are taken away.

C. In John 17:17-23 we see that sanctification issues in the genuine oneness because this sanctification keeps us in the Triune God; verse 21 says, "That they all may be one; even as You, Father, are in Me and I in You, that they also may be in Us":

    1. In order to be one, we need to be in the "Us," that is, in the Triune God.

    2. The only way to be in the Triune God is by the sanctifying truth that deals with all the factors of division.

    3. By being kept in the Triune God, we are one, but whenever we are out of the Triune God, we are divided immediately.

    4. We need to contact the Lord every morning, touch the living Word, and have the divine reality infused into our being; as we contact the Lord in this way, the factors of division are overcome.

5. When the factors of division in us are put to death by the sanctifying truth, we are brought into the genuine oneness, for sanctification keeps us in the Triune God.

6. Sanctification through the word of the truth results in the oneness of the Body of Christ, which is the enlarged oneness of the Triune God (v. 21).

D. There are four factors of division:

1. The first of these factors is worldliness; as long as we love the world in a certain aspect, that aspect of worldliness becomes a cause of division (vv. 14-16, 18; 1 John 2:15-17; 5:19).

2. Another cause of division is ambition; when we contact the Lord through the Word and allow Him to infuse Himself into us, the truth thus imparted into our being kills our ambition (cf. Isa. 14:13).

3. A third cause of division is self-exaltation; we should be willing to be nobody and to exalt Christ as the only Somebody, the One who has the universal preeminence (Col. 1:18; 2 Cor. 4:5; 3 John 9-11).

4. The fourth factor of division is opinions and concepts; we should not hold on to our opinion but simply pursue the Lord's goal: the recovery of Christ as life and as everything for the building up of the church (Matt. 16:21-24; cf. Rev. 3:14).

Day 5 V. **When we move out of ourselves and into the Father and into His glory, we are one and are even perfected into one (John 17:21-24):**

A. In ourselves we have the four factors of division; we cannot escape from these four things if we stay in the self.

B. To be sanctified is to move out of ourselves and into the Triune God and to allow Christ to live in us; in this way, we are perfected into one (vv. 21-23).

C. This sanctification takes place by the Word, which

is the truth, and by the Spirit, who is the Spirit of truth:

1. As we come to the Word every morning, outwardly we touch the Word, but inwardly the Spirit touches us; by the Word and by the Spirit, both of which are the reality, we are sanctified.

2. The more we touch the Word and the more the Spirit touches us, the more we move out of ourselves; we move from one dwelling place, the self, to another dwelling place, the Triune God.

3. Every day we need to make this move, for in the self there are worldliness, ambition, self-exaltation, and opinions and concepts.

4. If we continually touch the Word and allow the Spirit to touch us day by day, we shall be sanctified; that is, we shall move out of ourselves, our old lodging place, and into the Triune God, our new lodging place.

5. Once we are out of ourselves, we are sanctified, separated from the factors of division and separated not only unto God but also into God.

6. To have the genuine oneness, we must first move out of ourselves and into the Triune God (vv. 17, 21); then we must allow Christ to live in us (v. 23a):

   a. This perfected oneness is the real building; it is the growth in life (Eph. 4:16).

   b. To grow in life means that we move out of ourselves and into the Triune God and allow Christ to live in us; if we move into the Triune God and allow Christ to live in us, we can be one with the saints in any locality.

Day 6   D. "I in them, and You in Me, that they may be perfected into one" (John 17:23):

1. To be perfected into one means to be rescued from worldliness, ambition, self-exaltation, and opinions and concepts.

2. "I in them"—this means that the Son is living and moving in us.

3. "You in Me"—this means that the Father is living and moving in the Son.

4. In other words, while the Son lives and moves in us, the Father lives and moves in Him; by this twofold living and moving, we are perfected into one, and we express the Father in glory.

E. Ambition is implied in John 17:21; self-exaltation, in verse 22; and concepts and opinions, in verse 23:

1. In the Triune God there is no ambition, in the glory of the Father there is no self-exaltation, and in the place where Christ lives and reigns there are no opinions.

2. In the divine and mystical realm of the processed Triune God, ambition is swallowed up, self-exaltation disappears, and concepts and opinions are killed; here there is no evil of division in the Satan-systematized world (v. 15); instead, there is genuine oneness.

F. Genuine oneness is living in the Father, allowing Christ to live in us, and living in the Father's glory, His expression (vv. 22, 24):

1. We need to move out of ourselves and into the Triune God and remain in Him for the Father's expression, His glory.

2. The real building, the oneness, is possible only in the Triune God, and it is prevailing only when Christ lives in us; then we can express the Father in glory and experience the genuine oneness.

Morning Nourishment

John ...Jesus spoke to them, saying, I am the light of the
8:12 world; he who follows Me shall by no means walk in
    darkness, but shall have the light of life.

Eph. That the God of our Lord Jesus Christ, the Father of
1:17-18 glory, may give to you a spirit of wisdom and revela-
    tion in the full knowledge of Him, the eyes of your
    heart having been enlightened, that you may know...

In the Bible *truth* does not denote doctrine. It firstly means the
shining of the light, the expression of the light. In other words,
truth is light expressed. God never comes to us without shining
upon us. When God comes to us as light and shines, we immediately have the sense of truth, of reality.

Television is a very good illustration of this. Suppose there is a
parade in Washington, D.C. Without television, you could not be
on the West Coast and receive a vision of the parade. Although
you could read about the parade the next day in a newspaper, the
newspaper account would not make the parade real to you. Many
Christians today use the Bible like a newspaper, but they do not
have the vision of what is written in the Word.

Thank the Lord for the speaking that televises a vision to us!
...In the New Testament *truth* denotes this kind of heavenly television. Truth is not merely a report, not simply words written in
the Bible; it is a heavenly, spiritual vision televised into our being.
We all need to learn to differentiate the speaking that gives merely
a news report from the speaking that televises a vision into us.
(*Truth Messages*, pp. 16-17)

Today's Reading

Because we all need to see the heavenly vision, in Ephesians 1
Paul prayed that we would have a spirit of wisdom and revelation.

The difference between a newspaper and television is that
with the newspaper there is no light, only printed letters, but...
through light and electricity the vision is televised into us.

In the Bible, truth refers to the shining of the light. The Bible
contains many doctrines. However, when light from the Father in

the heavens shines upon the words in the Bible, these words immediately become truth to us. First we have the doctrine in printed letters, and then the heavenly light shines upon words of the Bible to show us the truth. Many read the verses about Christ dying for sinners merely as a newspaper report; they have nothing more than a doctrine about the death of Christ. But when, by the mercy of God, the light shines on these verses, they see the truth of Christ's death and are saved. Once they had the doctrine; now they have the vision and the reality.

Reality is the realization of what is real. The way to have such a realization of spiritual things is by heavenly television....There are a great many facts in the Bible. However, it is not adequate merely to read about these facts. By reading you receive doctrine. ...Along with this, you need the heavenly light to shine upon the facts. When the light shines, the doctrine is immediately changed into truth. In this way, you realize the real thing, the reality. Therefore, to know the truth we first need the facts and then the light that televises the vision of the facts into our being.

According to the Bible, the Spirit is called...the Spirit of reality (John 14:17). The Spirit of reality is the heavenly electricity by which spiritual things are televised into our being. The Bible also says that the Word is truth (John 17:17). All the spiritual facts are contained in the Word and conveyed by it. Christ is our holiness, Christ died for our sins, Christ is our life, the church is the Body of Christ, Christ is the Head of the church—all these are facts contained in the Bible. However, without the enlightenment from the divine electricity, these facts are mere doctrines. But when the Spirit shines upon these facts recorded and conveyed in the Bible, they become truth, reality.

All the divine facts are contained in the Word and conveyed to us through the Word. When the Spirit shines upon the Word, we have the heavenly television. The light shines upon the facts in the Word, and we know the truth. (*Truth Messages*, pp. 18-19, 22)

Further Reading: Truth Messages, msgs. 2-3

__Enlightenment and inspiration:__ _____
_____
_____
_____

Morning Nourishment

John **And you shall know the truth, and the truth shall set**
8:32 **you free.**
   36 **If therefore the Son sets you free, you shall be free**
       indeed.
17:17 **Sanctify them in the truth; Your word is truth.**

In 1 and 2 Timothy, two books dealing with degradation, truth is mentioned often because during a period of darkness there is the need for the shining of the light, the expression of the light.

Truth is the shining of light. Wherever there is light, there is God, for God is light (1 John 1:5). When the light shines upon us, it becomes the truth. In Romans 8 Paul encourages us to walk according to the spirit, but in John's second and third Epistles, also written in a time of degradation, John speaks of walking in the truth. Although in his other writings John emphasized life, in these two Epistles he spoke much about the truth [3 John 4]…. Whenever we are in a time of degradation and darkness, we need the shining of the light so that we may know how to walk in the proper way. (*Truth Messages,* pp. 8-9)

Today's Reading

In his second and third Epistles John emphasizes the importance of the truth. In 2 John 1 and 2 the apostle John speaks of loving in the truth, of knowing the truth, of the truth abiding in us, and of the truth being with us forever. In his third Epistle he again speaks of loving in the truth and especially of walking in the truth, saying that he has "no greater joy than these things, that I hear that my children are walking in the truth" (3 John 4). The emphasis on the truth in these Epistles indicates that they were written during a time of degradation when many had gone astray from the truth. Nevertheless, there were still a number who were walking in the truth.

In times of darkness we need to walk in the light (1 John 1:7). We have pointed out that truth always comes from the light, for it actually is the shining of the light. Today we need the truth, the shining of the light.

Now we need to see two functions of the truth. The first is found in John 8:32, which says, "You shall know the truth, and the truth shall set you free." The first function of the truth is to set us free. To be deprived of the truth is to be in bondage, in slavery, but to know the truth is to be released from slavery, to be freed. The second function of the truth is seen in John 17:17, which says, "Sanctify them in the truth; Your word is truth." On the one hand, the truth sets us free; on the other hand, it sanctifies us. It causes us to be saturated with the element of God. It is a very significant matter to have the truth, for it frees us from all negative things and saturates us with the divine element. The more truth we have, the more we are released from bondage and the more we are saturated with the element of God. Eventually the truth will cause us to be thoroughly sanctified and transformed. Hallelujah for the functions of the truth! How we need the truth in these days!

We must have both the Spirit and the Bible. Without the Bible, the Spirit cannot be the truth. We need to get into the Word so that we may have not only the Spirit but also the Spirit of truth. Eventually, this Spirit of truth is the truth itself.

In 3 John 4 the apostle John says, "I have no greater joy than these things, that I hear that my children are walking in the truth." In Romans 8, however, Paul tells us to walk according to the Spirit. Actually walking in the truth and walking according to the Spirit are one. When we walk according to the Spirit, we are walking in the truth; and when we walk in the truth, we are walking according to the Spirit. Never try to separate the Spirit from the truth, for these two are one.

Remember, apart from the Bible, the Spirit can be only the Spirit. Only when the Spirit is one with the Bible is the Spirit the Spirit of truth. How we thank the Lord that in His economy He has given us both the Spirit and the Word! Together these two constitute the Spirit of truth that sets us free and sanctifies us. (*Truth Messages,* pp. 12-13, 23)

Further Reading: Truth Messages, msg. 1

Enlightenment and inspiration: _____

_____

_____

_____

Morning Nourishment

John
16:13
But when He, the Spirit of reality, comes, He will guide you into all the reality; for He will not speak from Himself, but what He hears He will speak; and He will declare to you the things that are coming.

1 John
5:6
...The Spirit is the reality.

All three of the Triune God are related to the truth. The Lord Jesus, the Son, is the truth; the Spirit is the Spirit of truth; and the Father's word is truth. In the New Testament, especially in the Gospel of John, truth does not mean doctrine; it means the reality of the Triune God. We may have known that the Father, the Son, and the Spirit are all related to life, but we may have never seen that all three of the Triune God are also related to the truth.

The whole Bible is the word of God....Whenever we come to the Bible, we should have the consciousness that we are coming to God's expression, to God expressed....By means of the Bible, I can meet with God, talk to Him, and listen to Him. We all need to have such a conviction whenever we come to the Bible.

Christ, the Son, is also the truth,...[for] the Father's word is the Son, who is the expression of God....The Bible is the written Word and...the Son is the living Word.

All this is realized through God the Spirit....In the Gospel of John the Spirit is the Spirit of truth. The Father is embodied in the Son, and the Son is realized in the Spirit of reality. The Spirit is the realization of the Son as the embodiment of the Father. Therefore, the Spirit is the reality. The Spirit is also the word. John 6:63 says that the word is spirit, and Ephesians 6:17 says that the Spirit is the word. Hallelujah, we have the Word without and the Spirit within! (*Truth Messages*, pp. 46-47)

Today's Reading

Whenever we come to the Word with an open heart and an open spirit, we immediately touch both the Word and the Spirit as the truth....Two or three times every day we need to come to the Word....What a wonderful instrument the Word is for contacting the Lord! When we are disappointed or depressed, feeling empty within, we can open ourselves and come to the Word. After reading for a while, something within us rises up, and we enjoy the presence of the Lord. This is the experience of the truth, the reality. It is the Triune God in His Word being imparted into our being. This is the truth.

The Father is embodied in the Son, the Son is realized as the Spirit, and the Spirit is one with the Word. When we touch the Word, we also touch the Spirit. Then something is infused into our inner being. Whatever is infused into us in this way is the truth. Although this involves the acquisition of biblical knowledge, there is something living inside this knowledge. This is the Triune God realized by us and transfused into us through the Word. This is not merely the Word. It is the Word mingled and saturated with the Triune God and infused into our being. This is the truth that sets us free and sanctifies us.

We cannot sanctify ourselves. The more we try to be sanctified, the more involved we become with things that are common. But when the Word mingled with the essence of the Triune God is imparted into us as the truth, this truth sanctifies us....By contacting the written Word that is mingled with the living Word, something is transfused into us and works in us all day long.

This transfusion of the element of God frees us from such negative things as temper, jealousy, hatred, and pride. It sets us free from every kind of falsehood. This is real liberation, real freedom. As we are being set free, we are also sanctified, separated, made holy to God, not only positionally but also dispositionally. We become one with God because His very essence is being wrought into us. This is what it means to be sanctified by the Word of truth.

Daily we need to practice coming to the Word in this way. Like breathing, we cannot do this once for all; rather, it must be a continual exercise....When the Word is mingled with the living Spirit in our spirit, we are sanctified with the essence of God. (*Truth Messages*, pp. 47-48)

Further Reading: Truth Messages, msg. 5

Enlightenment and inspiration: _____

_____

_____

_____

Morning Nourishment

John
17:19-21 And for their sake I sanctify Myself, that they themselves also may be sanctified in truth. And I do not ask concerning these only, but concerning those also who believe into Me through their word, that they all may be one; even as You, Father, are in Me and I in You, that they also may be in Us; that the world may believe that You have sent Me.

Eph.
5:26 That He might sanctify her, cleansing *her* by the washing of the water in the word.

Sanctification through the word of truth results in oneness. The sanctifying word, the sanctifying Spirit, the sanctifying life, and the sanctifying God are all one. Therefore, if we are being sanctified, we can be nothing else but one. We are one spontaneously because all the factors of division are taken away.

In John 17:17-23 we see that sanctification issues in the genuine oneness because this sanctification keeps us in the Triune God. Verse 21 says, "That they all may be one; even as You, Father, are in Me and I in You, that they also may be in Us." In order to be one we need to be in the "Us," that is, in the Triune God. The only way to be in the Triune God is by the sanctifying truth that deals with all the factors of division. By being kept in the Triune God, we are one. But whenever we are out of the Triune God, we are divided immediately. (*Truth Messages*, pp. 49-50)

Today's Reading

[One factor of division] is worldliness. As long as you love the world in a certain aspect, that aspect of worldliness becomes a cause of division. It separates you from the brothers and sisters. Anyone who is worldly is through with oneness.

Another cause of division is ambition. Ambition is like a gopher that works underground in a hidden way to cause damage. Ambition undermines from within. We all must admit that we are ambitious. What can kill our ambition?...I can testify from experience...that when we contact the Lord through the Word and allow Him to infuse Himself into us, the truth thus imparted into our being kills our ambition. There is no other way for ambition to be rooted out of us. Day by day, the sanctifying truth kills the element of ambition within us. The germ of ambition is in our blood and needs the sanctifying truth as an "antibiotic" to kill it. If our ambition is not killed, there can be no genuine oneness.

A third cause of division is self-exaltation, which usually accompanies ambition....Such self-exaltation is like a serpent; it causes division among the saints. Therefore, in order to keep the genuine oneness, we must learn not to exalt ourselves.

If you are an elder or a leading one, you should not boast about this. Do not claim that you are somebody. It is better to be nobody. ...If you want to be somebody, you should not come to the church, for this is not the place for you....Christ is the only Somebody.... I thank the Lord that the vast majority of the saints are willing to be nobodies so that we can have the genuine oneness.

The fourth factor of division is opinion and concept. Opinion is like a scorpion. We should not hold to our own opinion, but simply pursue the Lord's goal: the recovery of Christ as life and as everything for the building up of the church. Those who have been with me throughout the years can testify that I do not insist on anything except Christ as life and as everything to us for the church. We should all be for this, not for our opinions and concepts regarding other things.

The four factors of division—worldliness, ambition, self-exaltation, and opinion—can be dealt with only by the sanctifying truth. Do you think that if you contact the Lord every morning, touch the living Word, and have the divine reality infused into your being, you will still be divisive? I do not believe it. As we contact the Lord in this way, the factors of division are overcome.

When the factors of division in us are put to death by the sanctifying truth, we are brought into the genuine oneness, for sanctification keeps us in the Triune God. Only by being in the Triune God do we have the genuine oneness. (*Truth Messages,* pp. 49-52)

Further Reading: Truth Messages, msg. 5

Enlightenment and inspiration: _____

_____

_____

_____

Morning Nourishment

John
17:24

Father, *concerning* that which You have given Me, I desire that they also may be with Me where I am, that they may behold My glory, which You have given Me, for You loved Me before the foundation of the world.

Eph.
4:16

Out from whom all the Body...causes the growth of the Body unto the building up of itself in love.

The Lord was in the Father, and He wanted His disciples to be in the Father also. In John 14:3 the Lord seemed to be saying, "I am in the Father, but you are not. By My crucifixion and resurrection, I shall bring you into the Father. Then where I am, you will be also." The Lord prayed for this very thing in John 17:24.... Eventually we shall be not only in the Father, but also in the glory. Firstly, the Lord brings us into the Father and then into the glory.

When we are with the Lord in the Father and in the glory, we are one. But when we are in ourselves, we cannot be one with others. In ourselves we are one only with ourselves, not with anyone else. If we desire to be one with others, we need to move out of the self and into God the Father. No one can make this move for us; we are responsible to do it ourselves. When we move out of ourselves and into the Father and into the Father's glory, we are one and are even perfected into one. (*Truth Messages,* p. 56)

Today's Reading

The way to make this move is by being sanctified. To be sanctified is to make the move out of ourselves and into the Father. If we remain in ourselves, we are not sanctified and thus we cannot be one with others. In ourselves we have worldliness, ambition, self-exaltation, and opinion. It is impossible for us to eradicate these things from our being....The world is actually yourself....The same is true of ambition, self-exaltation, and opinions and concepts. This is the reason we cannot escape from these four things if we stay in the self....The church life, however, is a building, and the real building is the genuine oneness. In this genuine oneness there is no room for worldliness, ambition, self-exaltation, or opinion.

The Lord Jesus knows our problem. In John 15:5 He said, "Apart from Me you can do nothing." He is the vine, and we are the branches. We must remain in Him, that is, abide in Him. To remain in Christ as the vine means that we move out of ourselves and into Him. Since the Lord is in the Father, we also may be in the Father by being in Him. In John 17:21 the Lord prayed, "That they all may be one; even as You, Father, are in Me and I in You, that they also may be in Us." This is the oneness in the Triune God. In order to be in the Triune God, we must move out of ourselves. John 17:22-23a says, "And the glory which You have given Me I have given to them, that they may be one, even as We are one; I in them, and You in Me, that they may be perfected into one." When we move out of ourselves and remain in the Triune God, Christ lives in us. In this way we are perfected into one.

Only by our being sanctified can we abide in Christ and can Christ live in us....According to [John 14—17], this is the proper concept of sanctification. The more we are sanctified, the more we are out of ourselves and in the Triune God.

This sanctification takes place by the Word, which is truth, and by the Spirit, which is the Spirit of truth. In these four chapters of John the Word and the Spirit are mentioned again and again. Actually, the Word and the Spirit are one....As we come to the Word every morning, outwardly we touch the Word, but inwardly the Spirit touches us. By the Word and by the Spirit, both of which are the reality, we are sanctified.

This perfected oneness is the real building....[According to Ephesians 4], real building is the proper growth in life. When we grow in life normally, we get out of ourselves and into the Triune God, and Christ lives in us. When this is our experience, we have the genuine oneness and we are perfected into one. When we are perfected into one, there is no problem with building. Wherever we go, we are one with the saints. But if we remain in ourselves, we shall have problems no matter where we may be. (*Truth Messages*, pp. 56-58, 61-62)

Further Reading: Truth Messages, msg. 6

Enlightenment and inspiration: _____

_____

_____

Morning Nourishment

John
17:21-23
That they all may be one; even as You, Father, are in Me and I in You, that they also may be in Us; that the world may believe that You have sent Me. And the glory which You have given Me I have given to them, that they may be one, even as We are one; I in them, and You in Me, that they may be perfected into one, that the world may know that You have sent Me and have loved them even as You have loved Me.

In His prayer in John 17 the Lord did not pray that the disciples would be brought into the Father, for He assumed that they were in the Father already. By being in the Father the disciples had the genuine oneness, but they still needed to be perfected in this oneness. The reason you may not have the boldness to say that you are in the glory of the Father is that you have not yet been perfected into one. To be perfected into one means to be rescued from worldliness, ambition, self-exaltation, and opinions and concepts. (*Truth Messages*, p. 77)

Today's Reading

As you read John 17:23, you may wonder what "I in them" and "You in Me" have to do with being perfected into one. Here the Lord does not say, "You in Me and I in them." This seems more logical than saying, "I in them and You in Me," for then the Father would be working in the Son, who would in turn be working in the believers to perfect them into one....According to our experience, I believe that it means that while Christ is working in us, the Father is working in Him....By this twofold living and moving, we are perfected into one.

Genuine oneness does not come from being taught or from holding certain doctrinal concepts. Real oneness comes from the Son living and moving in us with the Father living and moving in Him. Through this twofold living and moving we are perfected into one, and we express the Father.

As the indwelling Christ lives and moves within us with the Father living and moving in Him, we are rescued from our ambition, self-exaltation, and concepts. Sometimes when I am with the leading ones, I have the impression that they are too quick to express their opinion or to make decisions. This indicates that they have not been perfected into one. If we have been perfected, we shall not be bold in expressing our opinions or in making decisions. We would be restrained by the indwelling Christ, and we would spontaneously check whether what we are about to say is of Christ or of the self. This is the perfecting.

The Lord's prayer in John 17 reveals that we need to be brought onward from being just in the Father to being in the Father's glory. ...In Acts 1 the one hundred and twenty prayed in one accord (v. 14). Thus, on the day of Pentecost, they were not only in the Father, but also in the Father's glory. At that time there was no worldliness, ambition, self-exaltation, or concepts. Instead, there was only the expression of the Father. The genuine oneness had been perfected among them.

Oneness is possible and prevailing only where the Son is. The Son is in the Father and in the Father's glory....[Surely the] early disciples could boldly testify that they were in the Father and in His glory. Therefore, in the early chapters of Acts, the Lord's word in John 14 through 16 and His prayer in John 17 were fulfilled among them, for they had all been perfected into one.

We need to be delivered from a false understanding of oneness. Oneness does not mean that we have the same concept or that we merely gather together without dissension or division. Genuine oneness is our living in the Father and in the Father's glory. Whatever we think, say, and do must be in the Father and in His glory. When we live in this way, we are perfected into one. This is not a matter of outward behavior, but of inward reality, and we need to devote our full attention to it. Instead of living in ourselves—in our goal, purpose, ambition, feeling, or concept—we should live in the Father and in His expression. Then we shall be one where the Son is. (*Truth Messages,* pp. 77-80)

Further Reading: Truth Messages, msgs. 7-8

Enlightenment and inspiration: _____

_____

_____

_____

Hymns, #1081

1   Father God, Thou art the source of life.
     We, Thy sons, are Thine expression;
     In Thy name, our dear possession.
     Father God, Thou art the source of life.

       In Thy life, in Thy life,
       We have oneness in Thy life.
       In Thy life, in Thy life,
       In Thy life, O Father, we are one.

2   How we thank Thee that Thy holy Word
     With Thy nature, saturates us;
     From the world it separates us.
     Thank Thee, Father, for Thy holy Word.

       Through Thy Word, through Thy Word,
       We have oneness through Thy Word.
       Through Thy Word, through Thy Word,
       Through Thy holy Word we're all made one.

3   Oh, the glory of the Triune God!
     We're His sons, oh, what a blessing!
     We His glory are expressing—
     Oh, the glory of the Triune God!

       In Thy glory, in Thy glory,
       In Thy glory we are one.
       In Thy glory, in Thy glory,
       In Thy glory we are all made one!

Composition for prophecy with main point and sub-points: _____

_____
_____
_____
_____
_____
_____
_____
_____
_____
_____
_____
_____
_____
_____
_____
_____
_____
_____
_____
_____
_____
_____
_____
_____
_____
_____
_____
_____
_____
_____
_____
_____
_____
_____
_____
_____
_____
_____
_____

The First Great Pillar—Truth
(2)
Knowing the Divine Truth, the Divine Reality

Scripture Reading: John 1:14; 8:32; 14:6, 16-17; 15:26; 16:13-15; 1 John 5:6, 20

Day 1   **I. The divine truth, the divine reality, is the Triune God and His word (1 John 5:6):**

A. Reality is the element of God realized by us in the Son (John 1:14).

B. The divine reality is God, who is light and love, incarnated to be the reality of the divine things (1 John 1:5; 4:8; John 1:1, 14).

C. The divine reality is Christ, who is God incarnated and in whom all the fullness of the Godhead dwells bodily, as the reality of God and man, the types, figures, and shadows in the Old Testament, and all the divine and spiritual things (Col. 2:9, 16-17; John 1:18, 51; 11:25; 14:6):

1. Because Christ the Son is the embodiment of God, He is the reality of what God is (Col. 2:9).

2. The truth is the reality of the divine things, and this reality is Christ Himself (John 8:32).

3. The reality of the divine things came through Christ and becomes the realization of God to us (14:6).

D. The divine reality is the Spirit, who is Christ transfigured, as the reality of Christ and of the divine revelation; hence, the Spirit is the reality (1 Cor. 15:45b; 2 Cor. 3:17; John 14:16-17; 15:26; 16:13-15; 1 John 5:6).

Day 2   E. The divine reality is the Word of God as the divine revelation, which not only reveals but also conveys the reality of God and Christ and of all the divine and spiritual things; hence, the Word of God also is reality (John 17:17):

1. The Father's word carries the reality of the Father with it.

2. God's word is the reality, the truth, unlike Satan's word, which is vanity, a lie (8:44).

F. God, Christ, and the Spirit—the Divine Trinity—are essentially one; hence, these three, being the basic elements of the substance of the divine reality, are actually one reality (1:1, 14; 14:6; 1 John 5:6):

1. This one divine reality is the substance of the Word of God as the divine revelation.

2. The divine reality thus becomes the revealed divine reality in the divine Word and makes the divine Word the reality (John 17:17).

3. The divine Word conveys this one divine reality as the contents of the faith, and the contents of the faith are the substance of the gospel revealed in the entire New Testament as its reality, which is the divine reality of the Divine Trinity (Eph. 1:13; Col. 1:5).

Day 3

G. The divine reality is versus the lie, the vanity of the old creation, and the idolatrous substitutes of the true God (John 8:44; Eccl. 1:2; 1 John 5:20-21):

1. The devil's nature is a lie and brings in death and darkness (John 8:44):

a. With darkness is falsehood, the opposite of truth (1 John 1:6).

b. The satanic lie is the expression of the satanic darkness (Rom. 1:25; 3:4).

2. No matter how good, excellent, marvelous, and wonderful a thing may be, as long as it is of the old creation, it is part of the vanity of vanities under the sun; only the new creation, which is in the heavens and not "under the sun," is not vanity but is a reality (Eccl. 1:2-3; 2 Cor. 5:17).

3. Anything that replaces, or is a substitute for, the divine reality is an idol, and we should garrison ourselves against it (1 John 5:20-21):

a. Idols are the heretical substitutes for the genuine God and the vain replacements for the real God.

Day 4

b. We should be on the alert to guard ourselves from heretical substitutes and from all vain replacements of our genuine and real God (v. 21).

II. **We may know the divine truth, the divine reality, by being in the true One (v. 20):**

A. The Lord Jesus, the Son of God, has come and has given us an understanding that we might know the genuine and real God (John 1:14, 18; 1 John 5:20):

1. This understanding is the faculty of our mind enlightened and empowered by the Spirit of reality to apprehend the divine reality in our regenerated spirit (Eph. 4:23; John 16:12-15).

2. *Know* in 1 John 5:20 is the ability of the divine life to know the true God in our regenerated spirit through our renewed mind, enlightened by the Spirit of reality (John 17:3; Eph. 1:17).

3. Because as believers we have been born of the divine life, we are able to know the true God and the things of God (John 1:12-13; 3:6, 15; 17:3).

Day 5

B. First John 5:20 twice speaks of *Him who is true, the true One, the True:*

1. The term *the true One* refers to God becoming subjective to us, to the God who is objective becoming the true One in our life and experience.

2. The true One is the divine reality; to know the true One means to know the divine reality by experiencing, enjoying, and possessing this reality.

3. This verse indicates that the divine reality, which is God Himself, has become our reality in our experience; the God who was once objective to us has become our subjective reality (v. 6).

C. To be in the true One is to be in His Son Jesus Christ (v. 20):

1. This indicates that Jesus Christ, the Son of God, is the true God.

2. This also indicates that the true One and Jesus Christ are one in the way of coinherence; therefore, to be in the Son is spontaneously to be in the true One.

D. The word *this* in verse 20 refers to the God who has come through incarnation and has given us an understanding to know Him as the genuine God and to be one with Him organically in His Son Jesus Christ:

1. All this is the genuine and real God and eternal life to us.

2. This genuine and real God is eternal life to us so that we may partake of Him as everything for our regenerated being.

3. *This* refers to the true God and Jesus Christ in whom we are; it includes the fact that we are in this One, the true One, and implies that, in a practical sense, eternal life is the God in whom we are in our experience.

4. Therefore, the true God and eternal life include our being in the true One and His Son Jesus Christ; now in our experience the true One becomes the true God, and Jesus Christ becomes eternal life.

E. By being in the True, we know the divine reality intrinsically and experientially (v. 20; John 17:3).

Morning Nourishment

John
1:14
And the Word became flesh and tabernacled among us (and we beheld His glory, glory as of the only Begotten from the Father), full of grace and reality.

1 John
5:6
This is He who came through water and blood, Jesus Christ; not in the water only, but in the water and in the blood; and the Spirit is He who testifies, because the Spirit is the reality.

Truth is God, Christ, and the Spirit. Therefore, truth is the Divine Trinity. Actually the three of the Trinity are all one reality.

Having seen that truth is the Triune God, we may go on to point out that truth is also the Word of God as the divine revelation, which not only reveals but also conveys the reality of God and Christ and of all the divine and spiritual things. Hence, the Word of God also is reality (John 17:17). (*Life-study of 1 John*, p. 81)

Today's Reading

In John 8:32 the Lord says, "And you shall know the truth, and the truth shall set you free." *Truth* here is not the so-called truth of doctrine, but the reality of the truth which is the Lord Himself (14:6; 1:14, 17). Verse 32 says that the truth will set us free. But verse 36 says, "If therefore the Son sets you free, you shall be free indeed." This proves that the Son, the Lord Himself, is the reality. Since the Lord is the embodiment of God (Col. 2:9), He is the reality of what God is. Hence, truth, or reality, is the element of God realized by us. When the Lord as the great I Am comes into us as life, He shines within us as light, and this light brings the divine element as reality into us. (*The Fulfillment of the Tabernacle and the Offerings in the Writings of John*, pp. 230-231)

If we would understand the meaning of truth in the Bible, we need to go beyond the traditional and common understanding of what truth is. The traditional view concerning the truth in the Bible as correct doctrine is not accurate, and the common denotation of the word should not be applied to the word truth as found in the Bible.

The Greek word *aletheia* means truth or reality (versus vanity), verity, veracity, genuineness, sincerity. It is John's highly individual terminology, and it is one of the profound words in the New Testament. This word denotes all the realities of the divine economy as the content of the divine revelation, contained, conveyed, and disclosed by the holy Word.

According to the New Testament, truth is first God, who is light and love, incarnated to be the reality of the divine things— including the divine life, the divine nature, the divine power, the divine glory—for our possession, so that we may enjoy Him as grace, as revealed in John's Gospel (John 1:1, 4, 14-17).

Second, truth in the New Testament denotes Christ, who is God incarnated and in whom all the fullness of the Godhead dwells bodily (Col. 2:9), to be the reality of: a) God and man (John 1:18, 51; 1 Tim. 2:5); b) all the types, figures, and shadows of the Old Testament (Col. 2:16-17; John 4:23-24); and c) all the divine and spiritual things, such as the divine life and resurrection (John 11:25; 14:6), the divine light (John 8:12; 9:5), the divine way (John 14:6), wisdom, righteousness, sanctification, redemption (1 Cor. 1:30). Hence, Christ is the reality (John 14:6; Eph. 4:21).

Third, truth is the Spirit, who is Christ transfigured (1 Cor. 15:45b; 2 Cor. 3:17), the reality of Christ (John 14:16-17; 15:26) and of the divine revelation (John 16:13-15). Hence, the Spirit is the reality (1 John 5:6).

Now we can see that truth, *aletheia*, in the New Testament refers to God. Truth is God as the divine light and love incarnated to be the reality of all the divine things for our possession so that we may enjoy God as grace. This means that the very God is the truth, the reality, of the divine things for our possession. Therefore, we need to possess God as the reality and then enjoy Him as grace. Hence, the divine reality is actually God Himself. He is the reality of all the divine things. (*Life-study of 1 John*, pp. 78-80)

Further Reading: Life-study of 1 John, msg. 9; The Fulfillment of the Tabernacle and the Offerings in the Writings of John, ch. 24

Enlightenment and inspiration: _____

_____

_____

_____

Morning Nourishment

Eph. In whom you also, having heard the word of the truth,
1:13 the gospel of your salvation, in Him also believing, you
were sealed with the Holy Spirit of the promise.
Col. Because of the hope laid up for you in the heavens, of
1:5 which you heard before in the word of the truth of the
gospel.
John Sanctify them in the truth; Your word is truth.
17:17

Reality is Christ as God incarnate. Reality is Christ as the One in whom all the fullness of the Godhead dwells bodily to be the reality of God, man, the types, figures, and shadows, and all divine and spiritual things. In the Old Testament we have many types, figures, and shadows. Christ is the reality of them. In the Bible we also read of many divine and spiritual things, such as life, light, wisdom, and righteousness. Christ Himself is the reality of all these things. Therefore, when we read the word *truth* or *reality* in the New Testament, we need to realize that it refers first to God and also to Christ.

We have indicated that in the New Testament truth denotes the Spirit, who is Christ transfigured and also the reality of Christ and of the divine revelation. For this reason, in 1 John 5:6, John says, "The Spirit is He who testifies, because the Spirit is the reality." (*Life-study of 1 John*, p. 80)

Today's Reading

It is surely worthwhile for us to study thoroughly the meaning of truth in the New Testament....Truth, reality, is God, Christ, and the Spirit....[Let us] consider other aspects of truth according to the Word of God.

The fourth aspect of what the truth is, the Word, is actually the explanation of the first three aspects of the truth, the Father, the Son, and the Spirit. Therefore, reality is God the Father, God the Son, God the Spirit, and also the divine Word. (*Life-study of 1 John*, pp. 80-81)

In John 17:17 the Lord prayed, "Sanctify them in the truth; Your word is truth." The Father's word carries with it the Father's reality. When the word says, "God is light," it conveys God as light.

Hence, it is the reality, the truth, unlike Satan's word, which is vanity, a lie (8:44). (*Life-study of John*, p. 483)

The Triune God, who is the reality of everything, is revealed in the Word and conveyed to us by the Word. What is revealed in and conveyed by the Word is the content of our Christian belief and also the content of the New Testament. This content implies the real situation concerning God, man, the universe, man's relationship to God and to others, and our obligation to God. All these different realities are related to the unique reality, which is the Triune God Himself. Then through our experience of Christ this reality becomes our human reality, that is, it becomes our human virtue with which we worship God. Finally, truth refers to things which are true and real.

All the different realities revealed in the New Testament are related either directly or indirectly to the unique reality—the Triune God. Therefore, for us Christians the knowledge of what is true or real must come through our experience of the Triune God.

God, Christ, and the Spirit—the Divine Trinity—are essentially one. Hence, these three, being the basic elements of the substance of the divine reality, are actually one reality. This one divine reality is the substance of the Word of God as the divine revelation. Hence, it becomes the revealed divine reality in the divine Word and makes the divine Word the reality. The divine Word conveys this one divine reality as the contents of the faith, and the contents of the faith are the substance of the gospel revealed in the entire New Testament as its reality, which is just the divine reality of the Divine Trinity. When this divine reality is partaken of and enjoyed by us, it becomes our genuineness, sincerity, honesty, and trustworthiness as an excellent virtue in our behavior to express God, the God of reality, by whom we live; and we become persons living a life of truth, without any falsehood or hypocrisy, a life which corresponds to the truth revealed through creation and the Scripture. (*Life-study of 1 John*, pp. 91-92)

Further Reading: Life-study of 1 John, msgs. 10-11

__Enlightenment and inspiration:__ _____

_____

_____

_____

Morning Nourishment

Eccl. Vanity of vanities, says the Preacher; vanity of vani-
1:2 ties; all is vanity.

1 John And we know that the Son of God has come and has
5:20-21 given us an understanding that we might know Him
who is true; and we are in Him who is true, in His Son
Jesus Christ. This is the true God and eternal life.
Little children, guard yourselves from idols.

When we walk in the light, we see one reality after another.
However, when we are in darkness, nothing is real to us. On the
contrary, everything is empty, vain. When we are in darkness, we
do not have any reality because we do not see anything. Instead of
the sense of reality, we have the sense of emptiness and vanity.

When we dwell in God, we are in the fellowship. When we are
in this fellowship, we are in light. Then as we walk in the light,
Christ, the Spirit, the church, the Body, and the members of the
Body are all real to us. We may testify and say, "Praise the Lord
that I see Christ, the Spirit, the church, the Body, and the ground
of the church! How wonderful! All this is real to me." (*Life-study of
1 John,* p. 62)

Today's Reading

If we would be in the divine fellowship, we need to abide in God
as light, and we need to walk in the divine light. The divine light is
versus the satanic darkness. The real issue here is not a question
of right or wrong; it is a question of light or darkness.

Let us read all of 1 John 1:6: "If we say that we have fellowship
with Him and yet walk in the darkness, we lie and are not practic-
ing the truth." To lie is of Satan. He is the father of liars (John 8:44).
His nature is a lie, and it brings in death and darkness. With darkness is falsehood, the opposite of the truth. The satanic darkness is
versus the divine light, and the satanic lie is versus the divine
truth. As the divine truth is the expression of the divine light, so the
satanic lie is the expression of the satanic darkness. If we say that
we have fellowship with God, who is light, and walk in the darkness, we lie, we are in the expression of the satanic darkness, and

we do not practice the truth in the expression of the divine light. If we are in the light, we shall see the church as a reality. We shall also see the Body and the members of the Body as realities. We shall see that we are a particular member of the Body. But if we are in darkness, we may think that we are a great member of the Body, such as the shoulder, when actually we may be a small member, such as the little finger. This is another illustration of the fact that to be in darkness is to be in emptiness, vanity. But to walk according to what we see of the reality in the light is to practice the truth. (*Life-study of 1 John,* pp. 63-66)

The book of Proverbs stresses the wisdom that man receives of God through his contacting of God, wisdom that teaches man how to behave in his human life. Ecclesiastes stresses the vanity of vanities of all things under the sun, as realized by man through the wisdom received from God. No matter how good, excellent, marvelous, and wonderful a thing may be, as long as it is of the old creation, it is part of the vanity of vanities under the sun. Only the new creation, which is in the heavens and not "under the sun," is not vanity but is reality. (Eccl. 1:2, footnote 2)

In 1 John 5:21 John goes on to conclude "Little children, guard yourselves from idols." The word "guard" means to garrison ourselves against attacks from without, like the assaults of the heresies. "Idols" refers to the heretical substitutes, brought in by the Gnostics and Cerinthians, for the true God, as revealed in this Epistle and in John's Gospel and referred to in the preceding verse. Idols here also refer to anything that replaces the real God. We as genuine children of the genuine God should be on the alert to guard ourselves from these heretical substitutes and all vain replacements of our genuine and real God, with whom we are organically one and who is eternal life to us. This is the aged apostle's word of warning to all his little children as a conclusion of his Epistle. (*Life-study of 1 John,* p. 356)

Further Reading: Life-study of 1 John, msg. 7; Life-study of Ecclesiastes, msg. 1

Enlightenment and inspiration: _____

_____

_____

_____

Morning Nourishment

John
16:13-14
But when He, the Spirit of reality, comes, He will guide you into all the reality; for He will not speak from Himself, but what He hears He will speak; and He will declare to you the things that are coming. He will glorify Me, for He will receive of Mine and will declare *it* to you.

In 1 John 5:20 John continues, "And we know that the Son of God has come and has given us an understanding that we might know Him who is true; and we are in Him who is true, in His Son Jesus Christ. This is the true God and eternal life." The word *come* here indicates that the Son of God has come through incarnation to bring God to us as grace and reality (John 1:14) that we may have the divine life, as revealed in John's Gospel, to partake of God as love and light, as unveiled in this Epistle.

John says that the Son of God has given us an understanding so that we may know Him who is true, or know the true One. This understanding is the faculty of our mind enlightened and empowered by the Spirit of reality (John 16:12-15) to apprehend the divine reality in our regenerated spirit. In this verse to "know" is the ability of the divine life to know the true God (John 17:3) in our regenerated spirit (Eph. 1:17) through our renewed mind, enlightened by the Spirit of reality. (*Life-study of 1 John*, p. 348)

Today's Reading

The understanding spoken of in 1 John 5:20 involves our mind, our spirit, and the Spirit of reality. According to our natural being, our spirit is deadened, and our mind is darkened. Hence, in our natural being we do not have the ability to know God. How can someone with a deadened spirit and a darkened mind know the invisible God? This is impossible.

The Lord Jesus, the Son of God, has come and has given us an understanding that we might know the genuine and real God. He has come to us by the steps of incarnation, crucifixion, and resurrection. He accomplished redemption for us, and when we repented and believed in Him, we received Him. Now that we have believed in Him and received Him, our sins have been forgiven, our darkened mind has been enlightened, and our deadened spirit has been enlivened. Furthermore, the Spirit of reality, who is the Spirit of revelation, has come into our being. This means that the Spirit of reality has been added to our quickened spirit and has shined into our mind to enlighten it. Now we have an enlightened mind and a quickened spirit with the Spirit of reality, who reveals spiritual reality to us. As a result, surely we have an understanding and are able to know the true One. Before we were saved, we did not have this understanding. But the Son of God has come to us and has given us this understanding so that we may know God.

In John 17:2 and 3 we see that eternal life has the ability to know God: "Even as You have given Him authority over all flesh to give eternal life to all whom You have given Him. And this is eternal life, that they may know You, the only true God, and Him whom You have sent, Jesus Christ." Eternal life is divine life with a special function—to know God. In order to know God, the divine Person, we need the divine life.

Because as believers we have been born of the divine life, we are able to know God. In order to know a certain living thing, you need to have the life of that thing. For example, a dog cannot know human beings, because a dog does not have a human life. It takes human life to know human beings. The principle is the same with knowing God. The Lord has given us eternal life, the divine life, the life of God. The life of God certainly is able to know God. Therefore, the life of God, which has been given to us, has the ability to know God and the things of God.

The Son of God has come through incarnation and through death and resurrection and has given us an understanding, the ability to know the true God. This understanding includes our enlightened mind, our quickened spirit, and the revealing Holy Spirit. (*Life-study of 1 John,* pp. 348-350)

Further Reading: Life-study of 1 John, msg. 39; *The Collected Works of Watchman Nee,* vol. 40, "What Shall This Man Do?" ch. 10

Enlightenment and inspiration: _____

_____

_____

_____

Morning Nourishment

1 John This is He who came through water and blood, Jesus
5:6 Christ; not in the water only, but in the water and in
the blood; and the Spirit is He who testifies, because
the Spirit is the reality.

20 And we know that the Son of God has come and has
given us an understanding that we might know Him
who is true; and we are in Him who is true, in His Son
Jesus Christ. This is the true God and eternal life.

In 1 John 5:20 John twice speaks of "Him who is true."...To speak of God simply as God may be to speak in a rather objective way. However, the term *Him who is true* is subjective; it refers to God becoming subjective to us. In this verse, the God who is objective becomes the true One in our life and experience.

What does the word *true* mean? Here the Greek word translated *true* is *alethinos,* genuine, real (an adjective akin to *aletheia,* truth, verity, reality—John 1:14; 14:6, 17), opposite of false and counterfeit. Actually, the true One is the reality. The Son of God has given us an understanding so that we may know—that is, experience, enjoy, and possess—this divine reality. Therefore, to know the true One means to know the reality by experiencing, enjoying, and possessing this reality. (*Life-study of 1 John,* pp. 351-352)

Today's Reading

First John 5:20 indicates that God has become our reality in our experience. The Son of God has come through incarnation and through death and resurrection and has given us an understanding so that we may experience, enjoy, and possess the reality, which is God Himself. Now the God who once was objective to us has become our subjective reality.

John says that we are in the One who is true. We not only know the true God; we are also in Him. We not only have the knowledge of Him; we are in an organic union with Him. We are one with Him organically.

John says, "We are in Him who is true, in His Son Jesus Christ." To be in the true God is to be in His Son Jesus Christ. Since Jesus

Christ as the Son of God is the very embodiment of God (Col. 2:9), to be in Him is to be in the true God. This indicates that Jesus Christ the Son of God is the true God.

Let us consider in more detail John's word "we are in Him who is true, in His Son Jesus Christ." Notice that there is a comma after the word "true." In the original Greek text there is no punctuation at all. Hence, translators differ concerning whether or not a comma should be placed after "true."

Moreover, there is a question whether the phrase "in His Son Jesus Christ" is in apposition to "in Him who is true," or is an adverbial phrase. Some interpreters say that this phrase is in apposition; others say that it functions like an adverb. If this phrase is in apposition to "in Him who is true," the meaning would be that to be in the true One is equal to being in His Son Jesus Christ. If "in His Son Jesus Christ" is an adverb, then this phrase indicates that we are in the true One by being in His Son Jesus Christ.

Grammatically speaking, it may be preferable to say that "in His Son Jesus Christ" is not in apposition to the foregoing phrase, but is a modifier describing how we are in the true One. In this case, the meaning is that we are in the true One because we are in His Son Jesus Christ. In other words, we are in the true One by being in Jesus Christ. The reason we need to consider this matter is that it is vital to our spiritual experience.

After much study, I have come to the conclusion that either way we understand the function of the phrase "in His Son Jesus Christ," the outcome is the same. Whether this phrase is in apposition to the foregoing phrase or is a modifier, the result is the same. If the latter phrase is in apposition to the former, the meaning is that to be in the true One is equal to being in His Son Jesus Christ. This would also indicate that the true One and Jesus Christ are one in the way of coinherence. Therefore, to be in the Son is spontaneously to be in the true One. (*Life-study of 1 John*, pp. 352-353)

Further Reading: Life-study of 1 John, msg. 40; The Conclusion of the New Testament, msg. 397

Enlightenment and inspiration: _____
_____
_____
_____

Morning Nourishment

John   And this is eternal life, that they may know You,
17:3   the only true God, and Him whom You have sent,
       Jesus Christ.
14:6   Jesus said to him, I am the way and the reality and
       the life; no one comes to the Father except through
       Me.
1 John ...This is the true God and eternal life.
  5:20

Let us now go on to consider the last part of 1 John 5:20: "This is the true God and eternal life." "This" refers to the God who has come through incarnation and has given us the ability to know Him as the genuine God and be one with Him organically in His Son Jesus Christ. All this is the genuine and real God and eternal life to us. This genuine and real God is eternal life to us so that we may partake of Him as everything for our regenerated being.

We need to pay special attention to the word *this*. In 5:20 John does not say "He is"; he says "This is." This is the correct translation of the Greek. Furthermore, John uses the word *this* to refer both to the true God and to eternal life. By this we see that the true God and eternal life are one. (*Life-study of 1 John,* pp. 353-354)

Today's Reading

We have seen that we are in the true One and in His Son Jesus Christ. Doctrinally, the true One and His Son Jesus Christ may be considered two. But when we are in the true One and in Jesus Christ experientially, They are one. For this reason John uses "this" to refer both to the true One and to His Son Jesus Christ.

For someone who is not in the true One and Jesus Christ, They are two. But when we are in Them experientially, They are one. We have seen that to be in the true One is to be in His Son Jesus Christ. This means that in our experience of being in Them, They are one.

Moreover, when we are in the true One and Jesus Christ,

They are our true God and also our eternal life. First, John speaks of the true One and His Son Jesus Christ, and then he speaks of the true God. Here there may be some distinction between the true One and the true God. When we are in the true One and His Son Jesus Christ, the true One is called the true God, and His Son Jesus Christ is called eternal life. This means that first They are the true One and His Son Jesus Christ. But when we are in Them, They become the true God and eternal life.

We need a clear understanding of what "this" in 5:20 refers to. The word "this" refers to the very God who has become experiential to us through our being in Him. No longer are we outside of this God. Rather, we are in this God, and we are in the true One, in His Son Jesus Christ. Because we are in Them, God and Jesus Christ are no longer objective to us, and in our experience They are no longer two. When we are in Them, They become one to us. Therefore, John says that "this" is the true God, and "this" is eternal life. Who is "this"? "This" is the very God and the very Jesus Christ in whom we are. We may also say that "this" includes the condition of our being in God and Jesus Christ. Hence, the true God and eternal life include our being in the true One and His Son Jesus Christ.

We are in the true One and in Jesus Christ. Now in our experience this true One becomes the true God, and Jesus Christ becomes eternal life. Where are we now? Are we outside the true God and outside eternal life? No, we are in the true God and in eternal life. The word "this" includes this fact of our being in the true God and eternal life. Hallelujah, this is the true God and eternal life, and we are in this God and in this life! We know that we are in the true God and in eternal life because we are in the true One and in His Son Jesus Christ. (*Life-study of 1 John,* pp. 354-355)

Further Reading: Life-study of 2 John, msg. 2; *The Conclusion of the New Testament,* msg. 5

Enlightenment and inspiration: _____

_____

_____

_____

Hymns, #496

1   Christ is the one reality of all,
    Of Godhead and of man and all things else;
    No man without Him ever findeth God,
    Without Him man and everything is false.

2   All types and figures of the ancient time,
    All things we ever need, both great and small,
    Only are shadows of the Christ of God,
    Showing that He must be our all in all.

3   All things are vanity of vanities,
    Christ, the reality all things to fill;
    Though everything we may enjoy and own,
    If we're devoid of Christ we're empty still.

4   Christ is our real God, our real Lord,
    Christ is our real life, our real light;
    Christ is our real food, our real drink,
    Our real clothing, and our real might.

5   Christ also is the one reality
    Of all our doctrine and theology;
    And all our scriptural knowledge without Him
    Is just in letter and is vanity.

6   Christ, the reality of time and space,
    Christ, the reality of every stage;
    Christ is the one reality of all
    Thru all eternity from age to age.

Composition for prophecy with main point and sub-points: _____

The Second Great Pillar—Life
(1)
The Tree of Life

Scripture Reading: Gen. 2:9; 3:24; Rev. 2:7; 22:2, 14, 19

Day 1   I. **We need a vision to see that the Bible presents to us a picture of God in Christ as the tree of life to be our food; this is why the tree of life is mentioned both at the beginning and the end of the Bible (Gen. 2:9; Rev. 22:2, 14, 19):**

A. God's purpose in the creation of man in His image and according to His likeness was that man would receive Him as life and express Him in all His attributes (Gen. 1:26-27; 2:9).

B. The tree of life signifies the crucified and resurrected Christ, who imparts life to man and pleases and satisfies man in an edible form (v. 9).

Day 2   C. The tree of life is the center of God's economy; the carrying out of God's economy depends on the tree of life, for it is the way to fulfill God's economy (1 Tim. 1:4; Eph. 3:9).

D. The tree of life is the center of the universe:

  1. According to the purpose of God, the earth is the center of the universe, the garden of Eden is the center of the earth, and the tree of life is the center of the garden of Eden; hence, the universe is centered on the tree of life.

  2. Nothing is more central and crucial to both God and man than the tree of life (Gen. 3:22; Rev. 22:14).

E. The New Testament reveals that Christ is the fulfillment of the figure of the tree of life:

  1. John 1:4, speaking of Christ, says, "In Him was life"; this refers to the life signified by the tree of life in Genesis 2.

  2. The life displayed in Genesis 2 was the life incarnated in Christ (1 John 5:11-12).

3. If we put together John 1:4 and 15:5, we will realize that Christ, who Himself is life and also a vine tree, is the tree of life.

F. The enjoyment of the tree of life will be the eternal portion of all God's redeemed (Rev. 22:1-2):

1. The tree of life fulfills for eternity what God intended for man from the beginning (Gen. 1:26; 2:9).

2. The fact that the tree of life bears twelve fruits means that the fruit of the tree of life is rich and sufficient for the carrying out of God's eternal administration.

Day 3 **II. The Lord wants to recover the church back to the beginning—to the eating of the tree of life (Rev. 2:7):**

A. In general, Christians have neglected the eating of the tree of life and have lost sight of the fact that they have the right to eat the Lord (22:14).

B. God's placing man in front of the tree of life indicates that God wanted man to receive Him as life by eating Him organically and assimilating Him metabolically so that God might become the constituent of man's being (Gen. 2:9, 16-17):

1. God not only desires that man be His vessel to contain Him; He also wants man to eat, digest, and assimilate Him (Rom. 9:21, 23; John 6:57).

2. God wants to be digested and assimilated by us so that He can become the constitution of our inward being and that we will be one with Him and the same as He is in life and in nature (1 John 5:11-12; 2 Pet. 1:4).

C. The essence of the tree of life is in the water of life; if we would enjoy Christ as the tree of life, as the element of life, we must drink Him as the water of life, the essence of life (Isa. 12:3-4; John 4:14; Rev. 22:1-2).

D. Eating the tree of life, that is, enjoying Christ as our life supply, should be the primary matter in the church life (2:7; John 6:57).

Day 4   III. **Through the redemption of Christ, the way by which man could touch the tree of life, which is God Himself in Christ as life to man, has been opened again (Heb. 10:19-20; Rev. 22:14):**

A. As a fallen man, Adam was separated from the life of God and was not permitted to contact God as the tree of life (Gen. 3:1-6, 11-13, 22-24):

1. Satan's tempting man to take the tree of the knowledge of good and evil indicates that Satan wants to keep man from taking God as his life (vv. 1-6).

2. The significance of man's fall is that man was estranged from the life of God (Eph. 4:17-18).

3. God's prohibiting man by the cherubim and the flaming sword from taking the tree of life indicates that God's glory (signified by the cherubim), holiness (signified by the flame), and righteousness (signified by the sword) do not allow sinful man to abuse the life of God (Heb. 9:5; 12:29; Rom. 2:5).

B. When Christ's flesh was crucified, the veil was rent (Heb. 10:20; Matt. 27:51), thus opening the way for us, those who were alienated from God, who is signified by the tree of life, to enter into the Holy of Holies to contact Him and take Him as the tree of life for our enjoyment.

Day 5   C. "Blessed are those who wash their robes that they may have right to the tree of life" (Rev. 22:14):

1. Through Christ's redemption, which fulfilled all the requirements of God's glory, holiness, and righteousness, the way to the tree of life was opened again to the believers.

2. Those who wash their robes in the redeeming blood of Christ have the right to enjoy the tree of life as their eternal portion in the holy city, the Paradise of God, in eternity (v. 14).

IV. **In God's economy we are not only the eaters of the tree of life, enjoying the continually fresh fruit, but we are also the branches of this tree,** abiding in Christ, the tree of life, to enjoy the life-juice (v. 2; John 15:5):

A. The Bible reveals that the relationship that God desires to have with man is that He and man become one (1 Cor. 6:17):

    1. In His desire to be one with man, God created man in His image and according to His likeness and with a spirit to contact, receive, and contain Him (Gen. 1:26; 2:7).

    2. God desires that the divine life and the human life be joined to become one life.

    Day 6   3. This oneness is an organic union, a union in life—a grafted life (John 15:4-5):

        a. The grafted life is not an exchanged life—it is the mingling of the human life with the divine life.

        b. In order for us to be grafted into Christ, He had to pass through the processes of incarnation, crucifixion, and resurrection to become the life-giving Spirit (1:14; 1 Cor. 2:2; 15:45).

        c. As regenerated ones who have been grafted into Christ, we should live a grafted life, a life in which two parties are joined to grow together organically:

            (1) Since we have been grafted into Christ, we should allow the pneumatic Christ to live in us (Gal. 2:20).

            (2) We should live a grafted life by the mingled spirit—the divine Spirit mingled with the regenerated human spirit (1 Cor. 6:17; Rom. 8:4).

        d. In the grafted life, the human life is not eliminated but is strengthened, uplifted, and enriched by the divine life; the branch retains its essential characteristics, but its life is uplifted and transformed by being grafted into a higher life (Gal. 2:20; 4:19; Eph. 3:16-17a).

B. Christ as the tree of life is the embodiment of God as life to us (Col. 2:9), and we are united with Him organically; we not only eat Christ as the tree of life—we are united with Him, we are one with Him, and we are part of Him (John 15:1, 4-5; 1 Cor. 6:17).

Morning Nourishment

Gen. And God said, Let Us make man in Our image,
1:26 according to Our likeness; and let them have dominion...over all the earth...

2:9 ...Out of the ground Jehovah God caused to grow every
tree that is pleasant to the sight and good for food, as
well as the tree of life in the middle of the garden and
the tree of the knowledge of good and evil.

We need a vision to see that the whole Bible presents us a picture that God is the tree of life good for food to us. This is why the
tree of life is at the beginning of the Bible and at the end of the Bible
(Gen. 2:9; Rev. 22:2, 14). In between these two ends of the Bible are
many negative stories concerning the Lord's people being distracted, frustrated, and hindered from enjoying God as the tree of
life. All the positive stories in the Bible show us God's chosen people enjoying God as the tree of life in different aspects. (*The Tree of
Life*, p. 61)

Today's Reading

God's image [in Genesis 1:26], referring to God's inner being, is
the expression of the inward essence of God's attributes, the most
prominent of which are love (1 John 4:8), light (1 John 1:5), holiness (Rev. 4:8), and righteousness (Jer. 23:6). God's likeness, referring to God's form (Phil. 2:6), is the expression of the essence and
nature of God's person. Thus, God's image and God's likeness
should not be considered as two separate things. Man's inward
virtues, created in man's spirit, are copies of God's attributes and
are the means for man to express God's attributes. Man's outward
form, created as man's body, is a copy of God's form. Thus, God created man to be a duplication of Himself that man may have the
capacity to contain God and express Him. All the other living
things were created "according to their kind" (Gen. 1:11-12, 21,
24-25), but man was created according to God's kind (cf. Acts
17:28-29a). Since God and man are of the same kind, it is possible
for man to be joined to God and to live together with Him in an
organic union (John 15:5; Rom. 6:5; 11:17-24; 1 Cor. 6:17).

Created man was a duplication of God in God's image and likeness, but he did not have the reality of God or the life of God. Thus, he still needed to receive God as his life by eating of the tree of life so that he might have the reality of God to express Him (Gen. 2:9 and footnote 2). (Gen. 1:26, footnote 3)

As the Almighty God, Jesus is high, but when He came to us as food He was lowly. He was a loaf of bread. He was even the crumbs under the table (Matt. 15:21-27). The very Jesus who came to us as life in the form of food was not tall and great; He was small and lowly. Anything we eat must be smaller than we are; if it is not, we cannot take it into us.... [Instead], it must be cut into pieces small enough to eat. Thus, Jesus came to us as life in the form of food. He said, "I am the bread of life," and, "He who eats Me shall also live because of Me." God in the Son is the tree of life that is good for food. Day after day we can feed on Him. We can eat Him.

The tree of life typifies Christ who imparts life to man and who pleases and satisfies man (cf. John 15:1; Exo. 15:25). Christ imparts divine life into us, pleases us, and satisfies us. Many of us can testify of this. We can say, "Hallelujah! Jesus has imparted life to me. He satisfies me all the time." This is the tree of life. (*Life-study of Genesis*, p. 141)

The tree of life declares that God offers Himself to man in an edible form. The Lord Jesus brought this same message to man about Himself.

Why does the tree of life still appear in the closing book of the Bible? God wants to remind us that His intention for man will surely be realized. Man's disobedience caused only a temporary interruption. God's unchanging desire is to be received into His creature as food that the two may be one. His thought was not that man might behave decently and honor Him as the Creator with suitable worship. No! The tree was there declaring, "Here is God's life. Take this life into you and live by it." (*Life Messages*, vol. 1, pp. 235, 239)

Further Reading: The Tree of Life, chs. 1-2; Life Messages, vol. 1, ch. 26

Enlightenment and inspiration: _____

_____

_____

_____

Morning Nourishment

John I am the vine; you are the branches. He who abides in
15:5 Me and I in him, he bears much fruit; for apart from
Me you can do nothing.
1:4 In Him was life, and the life was the light of men.

God's intention positively is to express Himself through a corporate man, and negatively to deal with His enemy, Satan,
through this corporate man. At the end of the Scriptures there is
a city called the New Jerusalem (Rev. 21:2). God's image is expressed through that city (21:11; 4:3), and God's authority is exercised through that city (22:5; 21:24-26). That city is the very
expression and representation of God.

In Genesis 1 there is the purpose, the intention of God, but
there is not the way to fulfill God's purpose, the way to attain
God's intention. The way is not in Genesis 1 but in Genesis 2, and
what is the way? The way is the tree of life (v. 9). After the revelation of the words *image* and *dominion (authority),* there is the
word *life* in Genesis 2. How could we created human beings
express God if we did not have the life of God?...If God is life
within you and lives in you, it is possible for you to live God out, to
express God in a full way. The way to fulfill God's purpose is seen
in the tree of life. (*The Tree of Life,* p. 8)

Today's Reading

The tree of life is the center of the universe. According to the
purpose of God, the earth is the center of the universe, the garden
of Eden is the center of the earth, and the tree of life is the center of the garden of Eden. Hence, the universe is centered on the
tree of life. Nothing is more central and crucial to both God and
man than the tree of life. The tree of life in the garden was an indi-
cator that God desires to be our life in the form of food.

The New Testament reveals Christ as the fulfillment of the figure of the tree of life. Speaking of Christ, John 1:4 says, "In Him was
life." Since John 1:3 refers to the creation in Genesis 1, the mention
of life in verse 4 should refer to the life indicated by the tree of life in
Genesis 2. This is confirmed by John's mention of the tree of life

in Revelation 22. The life displayed by the tree of life in Genesis 2 was the life incarnated in Christ. The Lord told us that He Himself is life (John 14:6). Furthermore, John 15 reveals that Christ is a tree, the vine tree. On the one hand, He is a tree; on the other hand, He is life. If we put together John 1:4 and 15:5, we shall realize that Christ is the tree of life. The fact that He said in John 6 that He is the bread of life indicates that He has come to us as the tree of life in the form of food. Therefore, Christ, the embodiment of God, is the tree of life. (*The Conclusion of the New Testament*, p. 429)

Revelation 22:2 says, "And on this side and on that side of the river was the tree of life." The one tree of life growing on the two sides of the river signifies that the tree of life is a vine, spreading and proceeding along the flow of the water of life for God's people to receive and enjoy. It fulfills, for eternity, what God intended from the beginning (Gen. 2:9). The tree of life was closed to man due to his fall (Gen. 3:22-24), but opened to believers by the redemption of Christ (Heb. 10:19-20). Today the enjoyment of Christ as the tree of life is the believers' common portion (John 6:35, 57). In the millennial kingdom the overcoming believers will enjoy Christ as the tree of life as their reward (Rev. 2:7). Eventually, in the new heaven and new earth, for eternity, all God's redeemed will enjoy Christ as the tree of life as their eternal portion (22:14, 19).

Verse 2 also says that the tree of life produces twelve fruits, yielding its fruit each month. The fruits of the tree of life will be the food of God's redeemed for eternity. They will be continually fresh, produced every month, twelve fruits yearly.

That there are twelve fruits means that the fruit of the tree of life is rich and sufficient for the completion in God's eternal administration. Remember the significance of the number twelve: it is completion in God's administration for His economy eternally. Thus, the twelve fruits are for the eternal completion in God's administration for His economy. (*Life-study of Revelation*, pp. 748, 750-751)

Further Reading: The Tree of Life, chs. 3, 5; The Conclusion of the New Testament, msg. 41

Enlightenment and inspiration: _____

_____

_____

_____

Morning Nourishment

Rev. He who has an ear, let him hear what the Spirit says
2:7 to the churches. To him who overcomes, to him I will
give to eat of the tree of life, which is in the Paradise of
God.
22:14 Blessed are those who wash their robes that they
may have right to the tree of life and may enter by the
gates into the city.

O brothers and sisters, today we are in the last days. The Lord
wants to recover the church back to the beginning. That which
was in the beginning was so simple. There was a tree of life for
man to eat. Today, due to man's weakness and failure, the church
has become degraded, but it was not so in the beginning. In the
beginning it was all very simple. We thank and praise the Lord for
this. We all have to learn to be simple. Today is not the age of doctrines but the age of the spirit. Today is the age of eating the Lord,
drinking the Lord, and enjoying the Lord. (*The Lord's Recovery of
Eating,* p. 32)

Today's Reading

God ordained even before the foundation of the world that our
destiny, our future, would be to daily eat the Lord. What must
Christians do? Eat the Lord! What kind of Christian are you? We
are Christians who eat the Lord. What kind of church do you
have? A church that eats the Lord. Christians are people who eat
the Lord. This is the Lord's recovery. What is the Lord recovering?
The Lord is recovering the matter of eating Him. Christianity in
general has lost the matter of eating the Lord, and it has lost sight
of the fact that believers have the right to eat the Lord. The Lord
is recovering this today. (*Eating the Lord,* p. 14)

[The first step of God's procedure in fulfilling His purpose was
to create man as a vessel. Then] the second…was to place the created man in front of the tree of life, which signifies the Triune God
embodied in Christ as life to man in the form of food. God's placing
man in front of the tree of life indicates that God wanted man to
receive Him as man's life by eating Him organically and

assimilating Him metabolically, that God might become the very constituent of man's being. (Gen. 2:9, footnote 2)

God not only desires that man be His vessel to contain Him (Rom. 9:21, 23; 2 Cor. 4:7) but also wants man to eat, digest, and assimilate Him (John 6:57). When we eat, digest, and assimilate physical food, we are energized and strengthened. The food that we eat is dispensed into our blood, and through the blood into every part of our body. Eventually, the food that we have eaten becomes the fiber, tissue, and cells of our being. In the same way, God's eternal plan is to dispense Himself into us so that He becomes every fiber of our inward being. He wants to be digested and assimilated by us so that He can become the constituent of our inward being. (*The Divine Dispensing for the Divine Economy,* p. 9)

[Recently] I pointed out that Christ is the element of the Body and the Spirit is the essence of the Body. If we have only the element without the essence, what we have will be something merely objective, having nothing to do with us in our experience. No matter how much we may know about Christ as the element, if we do not have the essence, this element will not be related to us subjectively and experientially. But when we have the Spirit as the essence, we will also have Christ as the element. The essence of the tree of life is in the water of life. If we would enjoy Christ as the tree of life, as the element of life, we must drink Him as the water of life, as the essence of life. (*Life-study of Isaiah,* p. 75)

Eating the tree of life, that is, enjoying Christ as our life supply, should be the primary matter in the church life. The content of the church life depends upon the enjoyment of Christ. The more we enjoy Him, the richer the content will be. But to enjoy Christ requires us to love Him with the first love. If we leave our first love toward the Lord, we shall miss the enjoyment of Christ and lose the testimony of Jesus; hence, the lampstand will be removed from us. Loving the Lord, enjoying the Lord, and being the testimony of the Lord go together. (*Life-study of Revelation,* pp. 127-128)

Further Reading: The Tree of Life, chs. 7, 9, 11; Eating the Lord, ch. 1

Enlightenment and inspiration: _____

_____

_____

_____

Morning Nourishment

Matt.   ...Jesus cried out again with a loud voice and yielded
27:50-51   up His spirit. And behold, the veil of the temple was
split in two from top to bottom...
Heb.   Having therefore, brothers, boldness for entering the
10:19-20   *Holy of* Holies in the blood of Jesus, which *entrance*
He initiated for us as a new and living way through
the veil, that is, His flesh.

The tree of life is a symbol, signifying that God is life and the
source of life (cf. Psa. 36:9; John 1:4; 10:10b; 11:25; 14:6; 1 John 5:12;
Col. 3:4). This God became flesh (John 1:14) and was embodied in
Christ (Col. 2:9). The Gospel of John tells us that in Him was life
(John 1:4), He came that we may have life (John 10:10), and He is
life (John 11:25). Hence, the tree of life mentioned in Genesis 2
typifies Christ as the embodiment of God, who is the source of life.

God's original intention was that man should eat of the tree of
life (Gen. 2:9, 16). Because of man's fall, the way to the tree of life
was closed to man (Gen. 3:22-24). Through the redemption of Christ,
the way by which man could touch the tree of life was opened again
(Heb. 10:19-20). (*Truth Lessons—Level Three*, vol. 1, pp. 9-10)

Today's Reading

Satan's tempting of man to take the tree of knowledge indicates that Satan wants to keep man from taking God as his life
(Gen. 3:1-6). After man took of the tree of knowledge, God placed
cherubim and a flaming sword (Gen. 3:24) before the tree of life in
order to prevent man from taking of the tree of life also. God's prohibiting of fallen man by the cherubim and the flaming sword
from taking the tree of life indicates that God's glory (signified by
the cherubim), holiness (signified by the flame), and righteousness (signified by the sword) do not allow the sinful man to abuse
the life of God....The Lord judges by the sword, and the sword is
related to His righteousness. God's glory, holiness, and righteousness keep man away from taking God as his life. Fallen man has
lost his position to enter into God to take God as his life.

When Adam and Eve took of the fruit of the tree of knowledge, they chose the principle of independence. Their choice cut them off from the tree of life (Gen. 3:22-24). Through eating the fruit of the tree of knowledge, they were corrupted. They were no longer pure, because another source entered into them. This source was the nature and principle of Satan,…[which] is rebellion.…Because of this corrupting element, God is prohibited by His glory (signified by the cherubim), holiness (signified by the flame), and righteousness (signified by the sword) from contacting fallen man.… [Thus], the tree of life, signifying God as life, was temporarily kept away from fallen man (Gen. 3:22-24) until Christ came to accomplish redemption. His redemption satisfied God's glory, holiness, and righteousness. Therefore, through Christ's redemption the way was opened for fallen man to contact God.

The significance of man's fall is that man was estranged from the life of God (Eph. 4:17-19), signified by the tree of life. When the tree of life is mentioned in Genesis 2, the emphasis is on the tree itself.…Verse 9 says, "Good for food,…the tree of life."…Man's need was to eat the tree of life. Since the tree of life signifies God Himself, by eating the tree of life, man would have received God Himself as life. But by choosing the tree of knowledge, man became estranged from the life of God. Man's fall separated him from God as life, but Christ's redemption brings man back to God as life. (*The Triune God to Be Life to the Tripartite Man,* pp. 17-18, 13)

The tabernacle had two veils,…the screen at the entrance of the tabernacle, and…the veil separating the Holy Place from the Holy of Holies (Exo. 26:31-37).…The inner veil…typifies the flesh of Christ (Heb. 10:20b). When Christ's flesh was crucified, this veil was rent from the top to the bottom (Matt. 27:51), thus opening a new and living way (Heb. 10:20a) for us who were alienated from God, who is signified by the tree of life (Gen. 3:22-24), to enter into the Holy of Holies to contact God. (*Truth Lessons—Level Three,* vol. 1, pp. 164-165)

Further Reading: Truth Lessons—Level Three, vol. 1, lsn. 1; The Triune God to Be Life to the Tripartite Man, chs. 1-2

Enlightenment and inspiration: _____

_____

_____

Morning Nourishment

Rev. **And on this side and on that side of the river was**
22:2 **the tree of life, producing twelve fruits, yielding its**
fruit each month; and the leaves of the tree are for
the healing of the nations.
1 Cor. **But he who is joined to the Lord is one spirit.**
6:17

Revelation 22:14 says, "Blessed are those who wash their robes that they may have right to the tree of life and may enter by the gates into the city."...After his creation, man was put before the tree of life (Gen. 2:8-9), indicating that he was privileged to partake of it. But due to the fall of man, the tree of life was closed to man by God's glory, holiness, and righteousness (Gen. 3:24). Through Christ's redemption, which has fulfilled all the requirements of God's glory, holiness, and righteousness, the way to the tree of life is opened again to believers (Heb. 10:19-20). Hence, the believers who wash their robes in the redeeming blood of Christ have the right to enjoy the tree of life as their eternal portion in the holy city, the paradise of God in eternity (Rev. 2:7). (*Life-study of Revelation*, p. 758)

Today's Reading

In the Lord's recovery, we need to have the enjoyment of Christ every day. All day long we need to eat Jesus and drink of Jesus. While we are enjoying the foretaste of the tree of life, we are looking for the full taste to come. We are enjoying Him by eating Him as the tree of life and the bread of life.

We not only eat Him, but we also are united to Him. We are now His branches and are a part of the great vine. We enjoy the fruit of this vine, and we also enjoy the very life-juice as the branches. We are not only the eaters but also the branches. As the branches of the great vine, we can abide in Him, and He abides in us. What an enjoyment! We do not only eat Him, but we also abide in Him. (*The Divine Economy*, pp. 29-30)

The Bible reveals that the relationship God desires to have with man is that He and man become one. It is not simply that the two are united together. Rather, it is a oneness in which He becomes us and we become Him. He is our life, and we are His living.

This relationship is an organic one. If I make a table and glue or screw the legs to the top, the relationship between the legs and the top is not organic; there is no living connection. Nor are false teeth organically part of us, even though they may look just like our natural teeth; the false teeth are lifeless. (*Life Messages*, vol. 2, p. 295)

[The word for *breath* in Genesis 2:7 is] translated *spirit* in Proverbs 20:27, indicating that the breath of life breathed into man's body became the spirit of man, the human spirit (cf. Job 32:8). Man's spirit is his inward organ for him to contact God, receive God, contain God, and assimilate God into his entire being as his life and his everything. It was specifically formed by God and is ranked in importance with the heavens and the earth in God's holy Word (Zech. 12:1). (Gen. 2:7, footnote 5)

Even if our original human life had not been corrupted, God would not want it. What God wants is not simply His own life but His own life added into our human life. In other words, what God wants is two lives to be joined as one life. In the physical world, the grafting of branches is a simple matter which perfectly symbolizes this union of two lives into one life.

The highest standard of living for a Christian is to live the mingled life of a God-man. God's purpose is to work Himself into us to the extent that He becomes us and we become Him, that we and He become completely identical in life, nature, and image. This is the pinnacle.

When we called on [the Lord], the holy breath came into us. From that time on, God has been grafted into our life. This Jesus Christ who is in us is the embodiment of the Triune God. Moreover, this embodied Triune God has become a Spirit, who is the compound Spirit of life. He is diverse and all-inclusive....God's life has been grafted into the human life, and the two lives have been joined to become one life. This is like the grafted branches being joined to the tree. (*A Deeper Study of the Divine Dispensing*, pp. 70-71)

Further Reading: The Divine Economy, chs. 4-5; *The Experience and Growth in Life*, ch. 1

Enlightenment and inspiration: _____
_____
_____
_____

Morning Nourishment

John 15:4   Abide in Me and I in you. As the branch cannot bear fruit of itself unless it abides in the vine, so neither *can* you unless you abide in Me.

Gal. 2:20   I am crucified with Christ; and *it is* no longer I *who* live, but *it is* Christ *who* lives in me; and the *life* which I now live in the flesh I live in faith, the *faith* of the Son of God, who loved me and gave Himself up for me.

We have been grafted into Christ, yet this Christ is the God who dwells in unapproachable light (1 Tim. 6:16). Since we cannot touch Him, how can we be grafted into Him? This is why Christ needed to pass through various processes. The first process that He went through was His becoming flesh (John 1:14) to be the seed of David (Matt. 1:1), the branch of David (Zech. 3:8; Jer. 23:5; 33:15), that we might be grafted together with Him. (*The Experience of God's Organic Salvation Equaling Reigning in Christ's Life*, p. 51)

Today's Reading

A grafter knows that in order to have a successful grafting, both of the grafting parts need to be cut and die. First, the part to be grafted has to die, and second, the part to be grafted into has to die also. Only when both sides die can the grafting be accomplished. On Christ's side, one day, as the branch of David, He died on the cross; however, although He died in the flesh, He was resurrected in the Spirit (1 Pet. 3:18b). Through death and resurrection He became the life-giving Spirit (1 Cor. 15:45b). By becoming such a Spirit, Christ was ready for the grafting. On our side, as sinners, we need to repent and receive the Lord. Once we repent and receive Him, He as the life-giving Spirit enters into our spirit and puts the divine life in us.

After we have been grafted together with Christ, we should no longer live by ourselves; rather, we should allow the pneumatic Christ to live in us. Furthermore, we should no longer live by our flesh or our natural being; rather, we should live by our mingled spirit, a spirit grafted with Christ. Thus, first, we are united with Him; this is a union. Then we are mingled with Him; this is a mingling. (*The Experience of God's Organic Salvation Equaling Reigning in Christ's Life,* pp. 51-52)

Some Christian teachers regard the Christian life as an exchanged life. According to this concept, our life is poor and Christ's life is superior. Therefore, the Lord asks us to give up our life in exchange for His. We yield our life to Him, and He replaces it with His own life. However, our Christian life is not an exchanged life. It is altogether a matter of the divine life dispensed, infused, into our human life. This is a basic concept in the Scriptures.

Because our human life was made in the image of God and according to the likeness of God, it can be joined to the divine life. Although our human life is not the divine life, it resembles the divine life. Therefore, these lives can easily be grafted together and then grow together organically.

The Christian life is not a matter of exchange but a matter of grafting. A lower life, our human life, is grafted into a higher life, the divine life. The higher life swallows the defects and infirmities of the lower life. As this takes place, the higher life spontaneously enriches, uplifts, and transforms the lower life. How marvelous! This is not our doctrine or opinion; it is the divine revelation in the Word of God. Furthermore, this revelation can be supported by our Christian experience. (*Life-study of Romans,* pp. 658-659, 661, 665)

Christ as the tree of life is for the divine economy to dispense God Himself into you and me. As the branches of this great vine, we are abiding in Him, and He is abiding in us. Then there is a dispensing of God into us, a dispensing of life from the tree into the branches. The tree of life is the very embodiment of God as life to us. Now we are united to Him organically. As we abide in Him and He abides in us, this embodied God is dispensing Himself into us to make us God-men....Praise Him for the tree of life, the embodiment of God as life, to be eaten and enjoyed by us to make us men of life! (*The Divine Economy,* p. 30)

Further Reading: Life-study of Romans, msgs. 63-64; *A Living of Mutual Abiding with the Lord in Spirit,* chs. 1, 3

Enlightenment and inspiration: _____

_____

_____

_____

Hymns, #1145

1 God gave His Son to man to be
The tree of life so rich and free,
That every man may taste and see
That God is good for food.

Yes, God is good for food!
Yes, God is good for food!
We've tasted and we testify
That God is good for food!

2 We eat this feast and take God in,
And as we eat we live by Him,
For all the elements within
This feast are God Himself.

Yes, Jesus is our feast!
Yes, Jesus is our feast!
We eat this feast and live by Him,
For Jesus is our feast!

3 Christ Jesus is the food we eat;
He is our bread, He is our meat;
He is our life-supply complete;
We daily eat of Him.

We daily eat of Him,
We daily eat of Him.
He is our life-supply complete;
We daily eat of Him.

4 This feast is so enjoyable;
To men it's so available,
For God said whosoever will
May come and freely eat.

Yes, come and freely eat;
Yes, come and freely eat.
For God said whosoever will
May come and freely eat.

Composition for prophecy with main point and sub-points: _____

_____
_____
_____
_____
_____
_____
_____
_____
_____
_____
_____
_____
_____
_____
_____
_____
_____
_____
_____
_____
_____
_____
_____
_____
_____
_____
_____
_____
_____
_____
_____
_____
_____
_____
_____
_____
_____

The Second Great Pillar—Life
(2)
The Flow of Life with the Ministry of Life
out of and for the Magnificent House of God

Scripture Reading: Ezek. 47:1-12; 2 Cor. 3:6; 1 Cor. 9:11;
3:6, 9; 4:15; 3:2, 12

Day 1   I. **In order to participate in God's ultimate move, we need to experience the flow of life out of the house of God (Ezek. 47:1-12):**

A. God's ultimate move is His move in man to deify man by saturating man with all that He is in His life, nature, element, and essence for the glory, the expression, of God (2 Cor. 3:18; 1 John 3:2).

B. The water flows out from under the threshold (Ezek. 47:1):

1. In order for the water to flow, there must be a threshold, an opening (cf. Psa. 81:10).

2. If we draw closer to the Lord and have more contact with Him, there will be an opening that will allow the living water to flow out from the church (*Hymns,* #846).

C. The flow is toward the east (Ezek. 47:1):

1. The river of God flows in the direction of God's glory (cf. Num. 2:3; Ezek. 43:2).

2. If everyone in the church seeks and cares for God's glory, the living water will flow out from the church (John 7:18; 1 Cor. 10:31).

Day 2   D. The water flows out from the right side of the house
&   (Ezek. 47:1):
Day 3
1. In the Bible the right side is the highest position, the first place (cf. Heb. 1:3).

2. The flow of life must have the preeminence within us, becoming the controlling factor in our living and work (Rev. 22:1; Col. 1:18b).

E. The flowing is by the side of the altar, showing that

we need the dealing of the cross and a full consecration to enjoy the flow of life (Ezek. 47:1).

F. For the increase of the flow of life, we need to be
measured by the Lord as the man of bronze (40:3;
47:2-5; Rev. 1:15; cf. John 7:37-39):

1. To measure is to examine, test, judge, and possess (cf. Isa. 6:1-8; cf. Ezek. 42:20).

2. The four measurings of a thousand cubits,
which is a complete unit (cf. Psa. 84:10), indicate that as creatures we need to be thoroughly measured by the Lord so that He may
take over and thoroughly possess our entire
being (Ezek. 47:2-5).

3. The more we allow the Lord to examine, test,
and judge us to possess us, the deeper the flow
becomes; the depth of the flow depends on how
much we have been measured by the Lord
(cf. 1 John 1:5, 7).

4. The more we are measured by the Lord, the
more we are restricted and limited by the flowing of the grace of life until eventually we are
lost in and carried along by the flowing Triune
God as a river in which to swim; in one sense
we lose all our freedom, but in another sense we
are really free (Ezek. 47:4-6).

Day 4

G. The river causes everything to live (v. 9a):

1. Where the river flows, everything shall live
and be full of life.

2. The flow of the river produces trees, fish, and
cattle (vv. 7, 9-10, 12).

H. The river waters the desert and heals the Dead Sea
(v. 8):

1. The river waters the dry, parched land and
heals the death waters.

2. This watering and healing are for the purpose
of producing life.

I. The river is unable to heal the swamps and marshes
(v. 11):

1. A swamp or marsh is a neutral place, a halfway

place, a place of compromise and lukewarm-
ness (cf. Rev. 3:15-16).

2. For the flow of life and for the church life, we
need to be absolute.

3. "If you are in the Lord's recovery, be in the
recovery absolutely, not halfway...The Lord
Jesus desires and requires absoluteness...By
being absolute we will be in the flow, and the
flow will not be a trickle but a river to swim in.
Then everything shall live where the river
comes" (*Life-study of Ezekiel*, pp. 311-312).

Day 5 II. **Our enjoyment of Christ as the flow of life, the
life-giving Spirit, is for us to be sowers, planters, waterers, begetters, feeders, and builders
with the ministry of life for the marvelous organic building of God, the magnificent house
of God:**

A. A sufficient minister of the new covenant is a person who ministers life to others in order to help
them grow in life (2 Cor. 3:6).

B. A minister of life is a sower who sows spiritual
seeds:

1. In 1 Corinthians 9:11 Paul says to the Corinthians, "We have sown to you the spiritual
things"; *the spiritual things* refer to spiritual
seeds.

2. A seed is a container of life, and to sow a spiritual seed is to impart life in, with, and out of
our spirit.

3. The Lord Jesus came as a Sower to sow Himself as the seed of life into the human race
(Matt. 13:3, 37).

4. In the Lord's recovery we, as ministers of the
new covenant, need to be sowers who impart
life to grow and produce Christ in others.

C. A minister of life is a planter who plants Christ into
God's people (1 Cor. 3:6):

1. The believers, who have been regenerated in

Christ with God's life, are God's cultivated land, God's farm, in God's new creation (v. 9).

   2. In order for us to plant Christ into others, we need the genuine experience of Christ as life in our spirit.

D. A minister of life is a waterer who waters people with Christ (v. 6):

   1. Once we plant Christ into others, we need to water them with the water of life (Rev. 22:17).

   2. We may liken a waterer in God's farm to an irrigation system with a reservoir that supplies a farm with water; we should be a divine "irrigation system" with a reservoir of living water stored within us to water the church as God's farm.

   3. We need to have the genuine experience of Christ as the water of life and a living contact with Him so that we can be a channel of living water, a divine irrigation system, that can supply others with the water of life (John 4:14; 7:37-39).

Day 6

E. A minister of life is a begetter, a father, who imparts life to his children, whom he begets (1 Cor. 4:15):

   1. To beget is to generate spiritual children, to bring them forth, through the impartation of life.

   2. We need to have the divine "life germ" in order to impart the divine life into others so that they may be begotten as children of God.

F. A minister of life is a feeder; feeding is a matter of life; it differs from teaching, which is a matter of knowledge:

   1. To give milk to drink or food to eat is to feed others (3:2).

   2. What the apostle ministered to the Corinthian believers seemed to be knowledge; actually, it was milk (not yet solid food), and it should have nourished them.

3. The sound teaching of the apostles ministers the healthy teaching as the supply of life to people, either nourishing them or healing them (1 Tim. 1:10b; 6:3; 2 Tim. 1:13; Titus 1:9).

G. A minister of life is a builder who builds with gold, silver, and precious stones (1 Cor. 3:12):

1. Gold symbolizes God the Father in His divine nature, silver symbolizes Christ in His redemptive work, and precious stones signify the Spirit in His transforming work (this is versus wood, which signifies the human nature; grass, which signifies man in the flesh; and stubble, which signifies lifelessness).

2. Song of Songs portrays that in the proper church life, the perfected believers coordinate with the transforming Spirit to perfect Christ's loving seekers by ministering the Triune God to them for their transformation by the Triune God's attributes being wrought into them to become their virtues (1:10-11).

3. This is for the building up of the church as the organic Body of Christ to consummate the New Jerusalem for the accomplishing of God's eternal economy (1 Cor. 3:12; Rev. 21:18-21).

Morning Nourishment

Ezek. And the glory of the God of Israel was there, coming
43:2 from the way of the east...
47:1 Then He brought me back to the entrance of the
house, and there was water flowing out from under
the threshold of the house to the east (for the house
faced east); and the water flowed down below the
south side of the house, on the south of the altar.
1 John ...We know that if He is manifested, we will be like
3:2 Him because we will see Him even as He is.

The New Testament, a record of God's move, shows us that
God can never move apart from man. In the beginning of the
New Testament, God moved into man, gained man, and became
a man (Matt. 1:21-23; John 1:1, 14). He moved not only as God
and not merely as man; He moved as the God-man. This was the
reason that in the four Gospels the high priests, the elders, the
scribes, and the Roman officials did not know who Jesus was.
They could not determine whether His activities were the activities of God or the activities of a man. He was a mystery, for He
was God, yet man; He was man, yet God.

Athanasius, one of the early church fathers, said concerning
Christ, "He was made man that we might be made God," and
"The Word was made flesh...that we, partaking of His Spirit,
might be deified." This is the principle of God's move on earth.
God's move is in man and through man. God's move is to deify
man, making man God in life and in nature but not, of course, in
the Godhead. (*Life-study of Job*, p. 129)

Today's Reading

There is no mention of the flowing of the river [in Ezekiel]
before chapter forty-seven. The flow of the river depends on the
building. Whenever and wherever a group of believers is built up
in oneness as described by Ezekiel, there will be the flowing of
the river out of the building. If there is the building in your locality, the flow will come forth out from the building.

Ezekiel 47:1a says, "Then He brought me back to the entrance of the house, and there was water flowing out from under the threshold of the house to the east." In order for the water to flow forth, there must be a threshold, an opening, through which it can flow. This indicates that if we, through Christ, have more contact with God and draw closer to Him, there will be an opening which will allow the living water of God to flow out from the church.

The river issues forth from the house and flows toward the east (v. 1b). The east is the direction of the glory of the Lord (Num. 2:3; Ezek. 43:2). The flowing toward the east indicates that the river of God will always flow in the direction of God's glory. The river cares for God's glory.

Everything in the church life should be for God's glory. For example, in our preaching of the gospel, we should seek the glory of God. If our gospel preaching is for God's glory, there will be an outflow of living water. However, if we do not care for the glory of God, the flow will be limited. Everyone in the church should seek and care for the glory of God. Then the living water will flow out from the church.

Ezekiel 47:1c also tells us that the water flows down below the south (right) side of the house. According to the Bible the right side signifies the highest position. The flowing of the water from the right side indicates that the flow of the Lord should have the preeminence. We need to give the Lord the highest position, and we also need to give the flow of the Lord the highest position. Then the flow will be prevailing and become the controlling factor in our living and work.

The flowing is by the side of the altar (v. 1d). This indicates that the flow is always by the cross. If we do not have the dealing of the cross, the flow will be frustrated. If we would have the flow, we must have the dealing of the cross. We need to be willing to pass through the cross so that the flow may come forth. (*Life-study of Ezekiel,* pp. 303-304)

Further Reading: Life-study of Job, msg. 24

Enlightenment and inspiration: _____

_____

_____

_____

Morning Nourishment

Ezek. When the man went out to the east with the line in
47:3-5 His hand, He measured a thousand cubits; and He led
me through the water, water that was to the ankles.
Then He measured...water that was to the knees. Then
He measured...water that was to the loins. Then He
measured...*and it was* a river that I could not pass
through; for the water had risen, *enough* water to
swim in, a river that could not be crossed.

The main point here is the man with the measuring reed in
his hand (Ezek. 47:3). This man, who is the Lord Jesus Himself,
has the appearance of brass (40:3)....In typology brass, or copper,
signifies judgment and testing. The Lord Jesus was tested and
judged as a man, and because He was tested and judged, He is
now testing and judging. Because He was tested, He is qualified
to test, and because He was judged, He is qualified to judge. He is
the One with the measuring reed in His hand, fully qualified to
measure us.

To measure means to test, to judge, and to possess. When a sister is about to buy some cloth, she first examines the cloth and then
measures it. Whatever amount she measures she also possesses.
This indicates that to measure is to examine, test, judge, and
eventually take over and possess. (*Life-study of Ezekiel*, p. 305)

Today's Reading

The man came with a measuring reed in his hand to measure
the flowing of the river (Ezek. 47:3-5)....When this man first measured the river, there was only a trickle coming out from the
house. Then he measured a thousand cubits, and the flow became
deeper, up to the ankles (v. 3). Again he measured a thousand
cubits, and the flow became deeper, up to the knees (v. 4). After
this the man measured yet another thousand cubits, and the flow
became even deeper, up to the loins (v. 4). When he for the fourth
time measured a thousand cubits, the flow became a river which
could not be passed over, and the river became waters to swim in.

The Lord's judging and testing of us are not once for all. In

Ezekiel 47 the man measured not once or twice or even three times; he measured four times. In the Bible four is the number of the creature. The four measurings here indicate that as a creature we need to be thoroughly judged and tested by the Lord and then be fully taken over by Him.

To be taken over by the Lord completely is not easy to experience. We may think that we have been fully taken over by the Lord, but after a period of time we will realize that we still have some reservation. Then we will be tested and judged again, and after this we will have a further consecration to the Lord, saying, "Lord, take this and possess it." We may think that the Lord has taken over everything, but the Lord knows that He has gained us only to a certain extent. Therefore, some time later we may again realize that we have reserved and preserved very much for ourselves. Once again we will make our confession to the Lord and experience His testing and judging. Even after a number of years, we still may have not been fully possessed by the Lord, and thus we will again need to be measured, tested, judged, and possessed by Him.

Many among us have not yet given up their self-effort but are still trying to stand up on their own. They continue to struggle in their efforts to stand on their feet. This means that they are exercising their own effort to be an overcomer. Those who are in such a situation need to realize that they need more grace. They need a deeper flow so that they will give up trying to stand and instead will swim in the river. The best way for us to swim in the river is to put our trust in the flow of the river, forget our own efforts, and let the flow carry us along.

When we are being carried along by the river, we should not try to have our own direction. We should forsake our direction and move in the direction of the flow. However, the flow may be in one direction, but our intention is to move in the opposition direction. For this reason, the Lord often has problems with us. (*Life-study of Ezekiel*, pp. 305-306, 308-309)

Further Reading: Life-study of Ezekiel, msg. 26

Enlightenment and inspiration: _____

_____

_____

_____

Morning Nourishment

Ezek. Then He measured a thousand *cubits, and it was* a
47:5 river that I could not pass through; for the water had
risen, *enough* water to swim in, a river that could not
be crossed.
John He who believes into Me, as the Scripture said, out of
7:38 his innermost being shall flow rivers of living water.

Brothers and sisters, if we want God's life to flow out, we have
to be measured by Him. When He measures us, He starts from
the inside and works to the outside step by step. According to
Ezekiel, there are at least four steps in the measuring. After the
first thousand cubits were measured, the waters were to the ankles.
When feet are immersed in water, they cannot walk as freely as
before. The feet of those who have been taken hold of by God are not
so free. Many brothers and sisters prefer to walk freely by themselves; they do not want to be restricted by God's life. Therefore,
they do not want to be measured by God. Once a person is measured by God, however, his feet will not be free to walk about at will.
After the second measuring, the waters become deeper; walking
is even more of an inconvenience. The more you are measured by
God, the more you will find that it is inconvenient for you to
engage in your own activities. After being measured the third time,
the waters were up to the loins; the whole body was hemmed in
by the water. When a Christian reaches this point, he will lose
almost all of his own activities. He will be enlightened, judged,
and measured by the presence of God; God will take hold of him to
such a degree that he will be bound by life. Brothers and sisters,
this experience is precious. When you meet such brothers and sisters, you notice that their eyes do not turn much, their words are
not sharp, and their hands and feet no longer act freely. They are
immersed more deeply into God's life, and God has gained more of
their inward being. In the final step, the river of John 7 comes, and
the water becomes so deep that a man can swim in it. At this
point, one is fully carried along by the flow of the water,...[one is]
lost in God. This is the deepest step. (*The Collected Works of
Watchman Nee*, vol. 38, "Measure and Flow," pp. 472-473)

Today's Reading

When we experience the Lord's flow only in a shallow way, we can still walk by our own effort. But when the flow becomes deeper, reaching up to the knees, walking becomes much more difficult. We have grace, but the amount of grace we have is not sufficient, so we continue to exercise our own effort. As the flow increases, it bothers, restricts, and frustrates us. When the flow of grace rises higher, to the loins, this is the hardest time to be a Christian....We have grace, but we still need to exercise our own effort. This is a dilemma. The river of grace is with us, but it is not deep enough. But once the flow of grace becomes so deep that we cannot pass over, we will praise the Lord and begin to swim in the river. As we swim, we will no longer try to stand on our feet. Instead, we will abandon our self-effort and begin to swim in the river....As we are carried along in this way, we can easily follow the Lord and let Him lead us wherever He wants us to go. (*Life-study of Ezekiel*, pp. 307-308)

Brothers and sisters, being measured is the secret to having the outflow of the water of life. While you are in communion with God, He will measure you. Verbal consecration is still not true consecration. You can be sanctified and genuinely consecrated only after you are enlightened and measured by God. Having a heart for God and a heart to offer up everything to Him is still useless. You have to be enlightened, judged, measured, and sanctified before there can be real service. The water of life will flow deeper and wider as you are measured more and more. There will be the fruit of life wherever the water of life goes, and others will receive the supply of life. O brothers and sisters, may we be measured by God again and again so that His life will flow out as a river of living water, going deeper and farther as it flows. (*The Collected Works of Watchman Nee*, vol. 38, "Measure and Flow," pp. 472-473)

Further Reading: The Collected Works of Watchman Nee, vol. 38, "Measure and Flow," pp. 467-473

Enlightenment and inspiration: _____

_____

_____

_____

Morning Nourishment

Ezek. And every living creature which swarms in every
47:9-11 place where the river goes shall live, and there will be
very many fish when this water comes there. And *the
water of the sea* shall be healed, and everything shall
live wherever the river comes. And fishermen will
stand beside the sea from En-gedi even to En-eglaim;
it will be a place for the spreading of nets....But its
swamps and its marshes will not be healed; they shall
be left for salt.

Where the river flows, everything shall live and be full of life
(Ezek. 47:9). This river is the river of life, and only life can cause
things to live.

In this flow the trees live and bear sweet, delicious fruit every
month (v. 12). Also, the water brings forth an abundance of fish
(v. 9). Cattle are implied by the names of two cities—*En-gedi* and
En-eglaim (v. 10). *En-gedi* means "the fountain of the kid," and
En-eglaim means "the fountain of the two calves." These fountains
are for the young cattle, the kids and the calves. From all this we
see that the flow of the river produces trees, fish, and cattle.

With the flowing of the river, there is also fishing (v. 10). Fishing signifies the increase in numbers. If the number of people in
your local church does not increase year after year, this means
that there is no fishing, and no fishing means that there is no flow.
If we would have fishing, we must have the flow. We need a place
to cast out and spread our net. We need fishing in order to have an
increase in numbers. (*Life-study of Ezekiel*, p. 309)

Today's Reading

Ezekiel 47:8 says that the river flows toward the eastern region
to the sea. According to the map, this sea is the Salt Sea or the Dead
Sea. By the flowing of the river out of the house, the salt water of
the Dead Sea will be healed. This means that death will be swallowed up by life. When there is a rich and deep flow of life in a local
church, much death will be swallowed up by life. However, if there
is no flow in a particular church, that church will become a "dead

sea" full of salt. But if there is the flow of the river, deadness is swallowed up by life, and then the "dead sea" will be made alive.

Although the Dead Sea and the dry places can be made alive and deadness can be swallowed up by life, the marshes cannot be healed (v. 11). A marsh is a place that is neither dry nor flowing with water. Consisting partly of mud and partly of water, a marsh is neither wet nor dry. A marsh signifies a situation that is full of compromise. This means that wherever there is a compromising situation, there is a marsh. We should never become involved with any situation that is a "marsh."

Our stand concerning the church must be absolute. If you stand in a denomination, you should stand absolutely....If you stand on the ground of the church, you must stand absolutely. You should be either cold or hot, but you should not be lukewarm. To be luke-warm is to be in a marsh. If you give up the denominations and the independent groups yet are not absolute for the proper ground of the church, you are in a marsh. It is possible for one to be in the church life without being absolute. Such a person is a marsh.

If you are in the Lord's recovery, be in the recovery absolutely, not halfway. Come back all the way from Babylon to Jerusalem. If you stop halfway, you will become a marsh, and you will not have any flow, not even a trickle. Rather, you will have just enough water to make you "muddy." You will be a marsh, and a marsh cannot be healed. Throughout all my years in the Lord's recovery, I have never seen a marsh that was healed.

In Revelation 22:11 the Lord Jesus says, "Let him who does unrighteousness do unrighteousness still; and let him who is filthy be filthy still; and let him who is righteous do righteousness still; and let him who is holy be holy still." Here we see that the Lord Jesus desires and requires absoluteness. We must learn to be absolute. By being absolute we will be in the flow, and the flow will not be a trickle but a river to swim in. Then everything shall live where the river comes. (*Life-study of Ezekiel*, pp. 310-312)

Further Reading: Life-study of Ezekiel, msg. 26

Enlightenment and inspiration: _____

_____

_____

_____

Morning Nourishment

2 Cor. Who has also made us sufficient as ministers of a new
3:6   covenant, *ministers* not of the letter but of the Spirit;
      for the letter kills, but the Spirit gives life.
1 Cor. If we have sown to you the spiritual things, is it a great
9:11   thing if we shall reap from you the fleshly things?
3:6   I planted, Apollos watered, but God caused the growth.

A sufficient minister of the new covenant is a person who ministers life to others in order to help them grow in life (2 Cor. 3:6)....
[There are] six statuses of a competent minister of the new covenant as revealed in 1 Corinthians: a sower, a planter, a waterer, a begetter, a feeder, and a builder. These six statuses are related to the matter of life, that is, to our experience and enjoyment of Christ as the life-giving Spirit.

In 1 Corinthians 9:11 Paul says to the Corinthians, "We have sown to you the spiritual things." *The spiritual things* refers to spiritual seeds. A minister of the new covenant, a minister of the new testament, sows spiritual seeds. The first thing a new testament minister does is not to pass on doctrinal teachings but to sow spiritual seeds. A seed is a container of life, and to sow a seed is to impart life. Hence, sowing the spiritual things is a matter of life. According to Matthew 13, the Lord Jesus came as a Sower to sow Himself as the seed of life into the human race (vv. 3, 37). Likewise, in the Lord's recovery of the church life, we need to realize that we should not merely pass on knowledge or doctrines; instead, we should sow spiritual things. In the Lord's recovery we as ministers of the new covenant need to be sowers who impart life into others. (*The Collected Works of Witness Lee, 1970*, vol. 1, p. 577)

Today's Reading

To be a sower is much more difficult than to be a teacher. In order to be a teacher, a person simply needs to go to a Bible school where he may be trained to be a good speaker....However, in order to be a sower, one must have seeds of life that can grow and produce Christ in others. Such spiritual seeds are not mere doctrines or letters; instead, they are something of life in our spirit. They are spiritual things, things that are in, with, and out of our spirit. To acquire teachings is easy, but to obtain these seeds is difficult.

In 1 Corinthians 3:6 Paul says, "I planted." Planting is also a matter of life, for it involves sowing seeds, the containers of life, or placing herbs, plants, or trees in the ground, all of which are living things that grow. Verse 9 tells us that we, the believers in Christ, are "God's cultivated land," that is, God's farm. The believers, who have been regenerated in Christ with God's life, are God's cultivated land, a farm in God's new creation. Corporately, we as the church of God have Christ planted in us. In order for us to plant Christ into others, we need the genuine experience of Christ as life in our spirit. If we grow and produce Christ within us, we will have something of Christ to plant into others. Again, spiritual planting is not a matter of doctrines but of life.

In 3:6 Paul continues, "Apollos watered." We should not only be planters but also waterers. Once we plant Christ into others, we need to water them with the water of life (Rev. 22:17). Day by day we should water the dear saints, who are plants in God's farm that need watering. We may liken a waterer in God's farm to an irrigation system with a reservoir that supplies a farm with water. We should be a divine "irrigation system" with a reservoir of living water stored within us to water the church as God's farm. We need to have the genuine experience of Christ as the water of life and a living contact with Him. Consequently, we will have a fountain of life bubbling within us constantly (John 4:14), and we will be a channel of living water, a divine irrigation system, that can supply others with the water of life (7:37-39). We need to be waterers, those who are filled with the water of life and who water their fellow believers for their growth in life. If we do not have the sufficient experience of Christ as the living water, it will be difficult for us to water others. (*The Collected Works of Witness Lee, 1970,* vol. 1, pp. 577-578)

Further Reading: The Collected Works of Witness Lee, 1970, vol. 1, pp. 577-583

Enlightenment and inspiration: _____

_____

_____

Morning Nourishment

1 Cor. For though you have ten thousand guides in Christ,
4:15 yet *you do* not *have* many fathers; for in Christ Jesus I
      have begotten you through the gospel.
3:2 I gave you milk to drink...
10, 12 ...As a wise master builder I have laid a foundation,
      and another builds upon *it.* But let each man take
      heed how he builds upon *it.*...But if anyone builds
      upon the foundation gold, silver, precious stones...

In 1 Corinthians 4:15 Paul says, "In Christ Jesus I have begotten you through the gospel." To beget is to generate something, to bring forth something, through the impartation of life. Like the apostle Paul, who begot the Corinthian believers in Christ by imparting the divine life into them, we should be fathers who beget spiritual children by imparting the divine life into others. Begetting, unlike teaching, is a matter of life. We need to have the divine "life germ" in order to impart the divine life into others so that they may be begotten as children of God. (*The Collected Works of Witness Lee, 1970,* vol. 1, p. 579)

Today's Reading

Paul says, "I gave you milk to drink" [1 Cor. 3:2]. To give others milk to drink is to feed them. Feeding is a matter of life. It differs from teaching, which is a matter of knowledge. Instead of merely instructing others, we need to feed them....We need to feed on Christ to produce spiritual milk so that we may be able to feed our spiritual children. This is a genuine experience of Christ as life.

In order to practice the proper church life, we need the genuine experience of life....Paul was not only a father who begot spiritual children but also a mother who fed them. We need to be spiritually strong and healthy so that, like Paul, we may be able to beget spiritual children and adequately produce the spiritual milk to feed them....If the elders become fathers who impart life to their spiritual children and mothers who produce the spiritual milk to feed them, we will have a proper family life in the church as the household of God (Eph. 2:19). The unique way to practice the church life as a proper family life is through the genuine experience of life. The new covenant ministers as sowers, planters, waterers, begetters, and feeders should eventually become builders. In 1 Corinthians 3:10-11 Paul speaks of himself as "a wise master builder" who laid the unique foundation, Christ, for others to build upon. Then in verse 12 Paul speaks of building upon the foundation gold, silver, and precious stones. As we carry out the work of sowing, planting, watering, begetting, and feeding, Christ will grow in the believers. This growth of life in the believers will be accompanied by a measure of transformation in them. While the believers grow day by day, they will be transformed (2 Cor. 3:18; Rom. 12:2). As they grow as plants on God's farm, they will experience transformation, which produces gold, silver, and precious stones. Consequently, the believers will be not only mature plants, that is, full-grown men in Christ (Rev. 14:4, 15; Col. 1:28), but also gold, silver, and precious stones, precious materials for the building of God's house (Rev. 21:2-3, 11, 18-22).

If we would be builders who build with gold, silver, and precious stones, we need to be these precious materials. Gold signifies the divine nature of the Father, silver signifies the redemptive work of Christ, and precious stones signify the transforming work of the Spirit. In building the house of God, the builders are not separate from the materials of the building. In order to be builders, we ourselves need to be the transformed materials by being constituted with the Triune God. We should be both the builders and the building material of the house of God. If we ourselves have not been transformed into precious materials, we cannot help others be transformed into such materials. We ourselves first need to be the precious materials and be built into the house of God. Then we will be qualified to build the house of God with other believers as the transformed materials. (*The Collected Works of Witness Lee, 1970,* vol. 1, pp. 579-580)

Further Reading: The Collected Works of Witness Lee, 1970, vol. 1, pp. 577-583

Enlightenment and inspiration: _____
_____
_____

Hymns, #1115

1 We have come, we have come to the house of God;
  We have come to the house, whence outflows the flood.
  On the right, day and night, constant is its flow,
  Watering us and causing fruits of life to grow.

2 From the house, from the house flows this living stream,
  From the house, to the earth, with the life supreme.
  Yet more deep, Lord, we seek that the flow may be;
  Thus we must be measured and possessed by Thee.

3 Measure us, measure us, measure every day;
  Measure us, measure more, measure all the way,
  Till we know that the flow is a mighty flood,
  Sweeping over all the earth for Christ the Lord.

4 Take us through, take us through, take us through the flow;
  Take us through, through and through, everywhere we go.
  Flow increase, never cease, till we swim in Thee,
  Till we are immersed in God eternally.

5 All shall live, all shall live where the river comes;
  All shall live, really live, everywhere it runs.
  Let the fount from this mount life abundant bring,
  Till the deserts of the earth with churches spring!

Composition for prophecy with main point and sub-points: _____

The Third Great Pillar—the Church
(1)
The Church as the Kingdom of God

Scripture Reading: Eph. 2:19; 1 Thes. 2:12; Col. 1:13; John
3:3, 5; Rom. 14:17; Matt. 6:10

Day 1 I. **Ephesians 2:19 reveals that the church is the**
kingdom of God:
A. The term *fellow citizens* indicates the kingdom of
God (v. 19).
B. In Ephesians 2:19 Paul's main concept is that of
citizenship in God's kingdom.
C. All the believers, both Jewish and Gentile, are
citizens of God's kingdom, which is a sphere
wherein God exercises His authority (John 3:5;
Rev. 1:6, 9):
1. Citizenship in God's kingdom involves rights
and responsibilities, two things that always
go together.
2. We enjoy the rights of the kingdom, and we
bear the responsibilities of the kingdom
(22:14; Luke 14:15-24; 19:11-27; Matt. 24:14;
28:18-19).
II. **God has called us to enter into His kingdom;**
the kingdom of God is the realm for us to wor-
ship God and enjoy God under the divine rule
(1 Thes. 2:12):
A. The kingdom of God is a divine sphere for God to
work out His plan; it is a realm where God can
exercise His authority to accomplish what He intends (Matt. 6:10).
B. The New Testament preaches the gospel in the
way of the kingdom; the gospel is for the kingdom,
and the gospel is proclaimed so that rebellious sinners might be saved, qualified, and equipped to
enter into the kingdom (Mark 1:14-15; Matt. 4:17;
Acts 8:12).

Day 2 III. **The Bible first presents the kingdom and thereafter presents the church; the presence of the kingdom produces the church (Matt. 4:23; 16:18-19):**

LIFE

A. The life of God is the kingdom of God; the divine life is the kingdom, and this life produces the church (John 3:3, 5; Matt. 7:14, 21; 19:17, 29; 25:46):

1. The kingdom is the realm of life for life to move, rule, and govern so that life may accomplish its purpose, and this realm of life is the kingdom.

2. The gospel brings in the divine life, and this life has its realm, which is the kingdom; the divine life with its realm produces the church (2 Tim. 1:10).

3. The gospel of the kingdom brings forth the church because the kingdom is the life itself, and the church is the issue of life (Matt. 4:23; Acts 8:12).

Reality

B. The kingdom is the reality of the church; therefore, apart from the kingdom life, we cannot live the church life (Matt. 5:3; 16:18-19; Rev. 1:4-6, 9):

1. The reality of the kingdom of the heavens (Matt. 5—7) is the content of the church life; without the reality of the kingdom, the church is empty.

2. Since the kingdom life issues in the church life, as we live corporately in the kingdom life, we spontaneously live the church life (Rom. 14:17).

Authority

Day 3 C. Without the kingdom as the reality of the church, the church cannot be built up (Matt. 16:18-19):

1. The church is brought into being through the authority of the kingdom.

2. The keys of the kingdom are given to make the building of the church possible (v. 19; 18:18; cf. John 20:23).

3. When the kingdom of the heavens is able to assert its authority over a company of

believers, those believers can be built up into the church (Col. 2:19; Eph. 4:15-16).

IV. **The Father delivered us out of the authority of darkness and transferred us into the kingdom of the Son of His love (Col. 1:13):**

A. Through regeneration we have been transferred into the delightful kingdom of the Son of God's love—a realm where we are ruled in love with life (v. 13).

B. When we live by the Son as our life in resurrection, we are living in His kingdom, enjoying Him in the Father's love; here we have the church life (3:4; John 6:57).

Day 4　　C. Although the kingdom of the Son of the Father's love comprises the present age, the coming age, and the eternal age, the emphasis in Colossians 1:13 is on the kingdom of the Son of the Father's love in this age, the age of the church:

1. Because the Father delights in His Son, the kingdom of the Son of the Father's love is a pleasant realm, a matter of delight (Matt. 3:17; 17:5).

2. The church life today is the kingdom of the Son of the Father's love, which is as delightful to God the Father as the Son of God is.

V. **The kingdom of God today is a realm of the divine species, in which are all the divine things (John 3:3, 5):**

A. To enter into the divine realm, the realm of the divine species, we need to be born of God to have the life and nature of God, thereby becoming God-men in the kingdom of God (1:12-13).

B. We were regenerated of God to become the species of God and enter into the kingdom of God; now we are God-men in the kingdom of God as a realm of the divine species (3:3, 5).

Day 5　VI. **The genuine church is the kingdom of God in this age; today, the believers live the kingdom life in the church (Matt. 16:18-19; 18:17-18;**

13:44-46; Rom. 14:17; 1 Cor. 4:20; Eph. 2:19; Col. 4:11; Rev. 1:4-6):

A. Each time the Lord Jesus spoke of the church, He mentioned it in relation to the kingdom; this indicates how intimately the kingdom and the church are related (Matt. 16:18-19; 18:17-18):

1. Romans 14:17 proves that the church in this age is the kingdom of God.

2. *The kingdom of God* in 1 Corinthians 4:20 refers to the church life (v. 17), implying that in the sense of authority, the church in this age is the kingdom of God.

3. What Paul and his fellow workers were doing in the gospel work for the establishing of the churches was for the kingdom of God (Col. 4:11).

4. The word *kingdom* in Revelation 1:6 reveals that where the church is, there the kingdom of God is; the church represents the kingdom.

B. Although the church today is God's kingdom, we are in the kingdom in reality only when we live, walk, and have our being in the spirit, not in our natural man (Rom. 8:4; Gal. 5:16, 25).

Day 6

C. When the authority of God's kingdom is allowed to operate in us, righteousness, peace, and joy will characterize our daily life (Rom. 14:17).

D. As those who are under the dispensing of the Divine Trinity, we need to live a kingdom life in the church, growing and developing in the divine life until we reach maturity (2 Cor. 13:14; Mark 4:26-29):

1. After we have entered into the kingdom of God through regeneration, we need to go on to have a rich entrance into the eternal kingdom of our Lord and Savior Jesus Christ by experiencing the full development of the divine life as revealed in 2 Peter 1:5-11.

2. As a result of the growth and development of the divine life to maturity and of living in the reality of the kingdom in the church life today,

we will inherit the kingdom of God (1 Cor. 15:50; Gal. 5:21).

VII. **The church brings in the kingdom; the work of the church of God is to bring in the kingdom of God (Matt. 6:10; 12:22-29; Rev. 11:15; 12:10):**

A. All the work of the church is governed by the principle of the kingdom of God.

B. The church is responsible for bringing heaven's will down to earth and for carrying it out on earth (Matt. 6:10; 7:21; 12:50).

Morning Nourishment

Eph. So then you are no longer strangers and sojourners,
2:19 but you are fellow citizens with the saints and members of the household of God.

1 Thes. So that you might walk in a manner worthy of God,
2:12 who calls you into His own kingdom and glory.

Now that we are no longer strangers and sojourners, we are
fellow-citizens with the saints [Eph. 2:19]. The term *fellow citizens*
indicates the kingdom of God. All the believers, both Jewish and
Gentile, are citizens of God's kingdom, which is a sphere wherein
God exercises His authority. As long as anyone is a believer, he is a
citizen of the kingdom of God. This citizenship involves rights and
responsibilities. We enjoy the rights of the kingdom, and we bear the
responsibilities of the kingdom. These two things always go together.

In verse 19 there is the thought of intimacy, seen in the term
fellow citizens. As unsaved Gentiles, we once were far off from God
and the commonwealth of Israel, but now we have an intimate relationship with the saints. We are fellow citizens with the saints and
members of God's household. (*Life-study of Ephesians,* pp. 230-231)

Today's Reading

As worshippers of idols (1 Thes. 1:9), the believers were in the
kingdom of Satan (Matt. 12:26). Now, through the salvation in Christ,
they are called and have believed into the kingdom of God [1 Thes.
2:12], which is the sphere for them to worship and enjoy God under
the divine ruling with a view of entering into God's glory. God's
glory goes with His kingdom. (*Life-study of 1 Thessalonians,* p. 104)

Much of today's gospel preaching gives people the impression
that the gospel is only for soul winning, for transferring people out
of hell into heaven, for helping people have peace, joy, and eternal
blessing. In the New Testament, however, we have a different
impression concerning the gospel. When the Lord Jesus preached
the gospel, He spoke concerning the kingdom of God, and He told
them to repent for the kingdom.

We need to see the crucial matter that the intrinsic essence of
the gospel is the kingdom. The gospel is preached for the kingdom,

and the kingdom is a divine sphere for God to work out His plan, a realm where God can exercise His authority to accomplish what He intends. The only way for God to reach His goal is through the kingdom. (*Life-study of Mark*, p. 120)

The whole New Testament is on the kingdom. What is the first item of the preaching in the New Testament? It is the kingdom. The kingdom is preached in the opening chapters of the Gospels. ...The New Testament does not say, "Repent, for heaven is ready for you." It says, "Repent, for the kingdom of the heavens has drawn near" (Matt. 3:2; 4:17). Today people hear thousands of gospel messages. Have you ever heard a gospel message telling people to repent because the kingdom is coming?...When Christians preach the gospel nowadays, most of them always talk about sin, heaven, and hell. Hardly anyone speaks about the gospel as related to the kingdom. But in its first preaching of the gospel, the New Testament tells us to repent for the kingdom.

The gospel is for the kingdom. The purpose of the preaching of the gospel is that men might enter into the kingdom. The gospel is proclaimed that people might be saved, qualified, and equipped to enter into the kingdom. Regeneration is for the kingdom (John 3:3, 5). If you have not been regenerated, you cannot enter into the kingdom of God. Have you been saved, washed in the blood, and regenerated? For what purpose? Before I came into the church life, I was told that we had to be saved, washed, and regenerated that we might go to heaven. In the church, we have seen something higher—that we have been saved, washed, and regenerated for the church (Eph. 5:25, 23; Acts 20:28). The gospel of the kingdom brings the rebellious sinners into the church. But now we need to see what is the reality of the church. The reality of the church is the kingdom. If you have been saved, washed, and regenerated for the church, it means that you have experienced these things for the reality of the kingdom. (*Life-study of Genesis*, p. 471)

Further Reading: Life-study of Mark, msg. 13; *Life-study of Genesis*, msg. 35

Enlightenment and inspiration: _____

_____

_____

_____

Morning Nourishment

John Jesus answered, Truly, truly, I say to you, Unless one
3:5 is born of water and the Spirit, he cannot enter into
the kingdom of God.

Rom. For the kingdom of God is not eating and drinking,
14:17 but righteousness and peace and joy in the Holy
Spirit.

The Bible first presents the kingdom and thereafter presents
the church. Where the kingdom of heaven is in authority, there a
church will be built up. A church comes into being where a company of people accept the government of heaven. So it would
appear to be the presence of the kingdom that produces the
church. But the New Testament goes beyond that. That is only
one half of the New Testament revelation; the other half is this—
the church brings in the kingdom. (*The Kingdom and the Church*,
pp. 24-25)

Today's Reading

Although the church and the kingdom are interrelated, there
is nonetheless a difference between them. Because any kind of life
is a kingdom, the kingdom is the life itself. For example, the animal life is the animal kingdom, and the human life is the human
kingdom. In the same principle, the life of God is the kingdom of
God. The church, however, is not the life, nor is the life the church.
Rather, the church is the product of life. The divine life is the kingdom, and this life produces the church.

The New Testament concept is that the gospel brings in the
kingdom. The gospel does not bring in the church, but the gospel
brings forth the church. The gospel brings in the kingdom of God,
and the gospel also brings forth the church of God. For this reason, in the New Testament the gospel is called the gospel of the
kingdom (Matt. 4:23; 9:35; 24:14).

Without the kingdom as the reality of life, the church cannot
be produced or built up. To produce the church and to build up the
church, we need the kingdom. The kingdom is the reality of
the church. We cannot say, however, that the church is the reality

of the kingdom. We can say only that the kingdom is the reality of the church.

Where the reality of the kingdom is lacking, there the building of the church will be lacking. A believer who does not live in the reality of the kingdom can at best be a saved person; he cannot be built into the structure of the church.

In the first preaching of the New Testament gospel, people were told to repent because the kingdom of the heavens had drawn near (Matt. 3:2; 4:17; 10:7). This meant that the time had come for God to dispense Himself as life into people. The gospel brings God as life, and this life is the kingdom. The kingdom is the realm of life for life to move, work, rule, and govern so that life may accomplish its purpose. The kingdom as the realm of life is actually the life itself. The gospel brings in the divine life, and the divine life has its realm. This is the kingdom. The divine life with its realm produces the church.

Because the kingdom is the reality of the church,...we cannot live the church life apart from the proper kingdom life. This is why we have emphasized the fact that the gospel preached at the beginning of the New Testament concerns not salvation but the kingdom. To enter the kingdom of God is to be regenerated. We may talk about regeneration without realizing that regeneration is for the entry into the kingdom....When God regenerated us, He regenerated us into His kingdom.

We need to be deeply impressed with the fact that the reality of the kingdom of the heavens is the content of the church life. This means that without the reality of the kingdom, the church is empty.

It is crucial for us to see that we experience the dispensing of the Divine Trinity corporately by living in the kingdom. As we live corporately in the kingdom life, we spontaneously live the church life. The kingdom life issues in the church life. (*The Conclusion of the New Testament*, pp. 1740-1741, 1743)

Further Reading: Elders' Training, Book 2: The Vision of the Lord's Recovery, ch. 4; *The Kingdom*, chs. 1-2

Enlightenment and inspiration: _____

_____

_____

Morning Nourishment

Matt. Truly I say to you, Whatever you bind on the earth shall
18:18 have been bound in heaven, and whatever you loose on
the earth shall have been loosed in heaven.
Col. Who delivered us out of the authority of darkness and
1:13 transferred *us* into the kingdom of the Son of His love.

The kingdom is…life's practicality….If we live the divine life, if
we live Christ as life, the practicality of this life is the kingdom.
When people come among us they would see a kingdom….In the
church, we are the believers living, moving, and acting in the divine
life. As a result, there is an expression of this divine life. The expression of this divine life is the kingdom, the practicality of this life,
and the practicality of this divine life is in the church. Now we can
see that the kingdom is the reality of the church life. (*Elders' Training, Book 2: The Vision of the Lord's Recovery*, pp. 48-49)

Today's Reading

When the Lord said, "Upon this rock I will build my church,"
He immediately added, "I will give to you the keys of the kingdom
of the heavens" [Matt. 16:18-19]. The keys of the kingdom are
given to make the building of the church possible. Where the authority of the kingdom is absent, there the building of the church will
be lacking. Anyone who refuses to submit to the authority of the
kingdom can at best be a saved person; he will never be built into
the structure of the church.

Because the kingdom of heaven is able to assert its authority
over a company of men, that company of men can be built up into
a church. It is necessary at this point to recapitulate. *Why* was the
church brought into being? For the purpose of bringing in the
kingdom! *How* was the church brought into being? By means of
the authority of the kingdom! God's purpose was to bring His
heavenly dominion to the earth, and apart from the church, His
goal could not be attained. He needed a people who would subject
themselves to the dominion of heaven, so that under that dominion they might be built up into the church. That is what Matthew
16 reveals. (*The Kingdom and the Church*, pp. 24, 27)

Our Father has delivered us from the authority of darkness and transferred us into the kingdom of the Son of His love. Here we are restricted by the divine love in the divine life. Instead of ordinances, observances, religion, or isms, we have Christ and Christ alone. If we see this, there will be no disputes or divisions in the church life. (*Life-study of Colossians,* p. 34)

The church life today is the kingdom of the Son of God's love which is as delightful to God the Father as the Son of God is. We, the believers, all have been transferred into this delightful kingdom of the Son of God's love. God the Father loves the delightful part of the kingdom just as He loves His delightful Son as His own. So, the church, as the delightful part of the divine kingdom, is considered a great blessing to God's redeemed people by the apostle Paul in the book of Colossians, a book which is on Christ as the all-inclusive portion of God's people (Col. 1:12).

John 3:5 indicates that it is through regeneration that all the believers have been transferred into the kingdom of the Son of God's love. Through regeneration we have been brought out of the darkness of Satan into this delightful aspect of the kingdom. (*The Conclusion of the New Testament,* pp. 2583-2584)

The Son in resurrection (1 Pet. 1:3; Rom. 6:4-5) is now the life-giving Spirit (1 Cor. 15:45b). He rules us in His resurrection life with love. This is the kingdom of the Son of the Father's love. When we live by the Son as our life in resurrection, we are living in His kingdom, enjoying Him in the Father's love.

We have been transferred into a realm where we are ruled in love with life. Here, under the heavenly ruling and restriction, we have genuine freedom, the proper freedom in love, with life, and under light. This is what it means to be delivered out of the authority of darkness and transferred into the kingdom of the Son of His love. Here in this kingdom we enjoy Christ and have the church life. (*Life-study of Colossians,* p. 35)

Further Reading: The Kingdom and the Church, chs. 1-3; *The Conclusion of the New Testament,* msg. 209

Enlightenment and inspiration: _____

_____

_____

_____

Morning Nourishment

Matt. And behold, a voice out of the heavens, saying, This
3:17 is My Son, the Beloved, in whom I have found My
delight.

John But as many as received Him, to them He gave the
1:12-13 authority to become children of God, to those who
believe into His name, who were begotten not of
blood, nor of the will of the flesh, nor of the will of
man, but of God.

The kingdom of the Son of God's love comprises three ages: the
present age, in which the church is; the coming age, in which the
millennial kingdom will be; and the eternal age with the New
Jerusalem in the new heaven and the new earth. These three
aspects of the kingdom are considered by Paul in Colossians 1:13
as the kingdom of the Son of God's love.

The words *the Son of God* are a delight to the Father's ears.
When the Lord Jesus was baptized, the Father declared, "This is
My Son, the Beloved, in whom I have found My delight" (Matt.
3:17). When the Lord was transfigured, the Father made the same
declaration (Matt. 17:5). Because the Father delights in His Son,
the kingdom of the Son of the Father's love is a pleasant thing,
a matter of delight. This is the reason it comprises only three sections—the section of the church life, the section of the heavenly
part of the kingdom of the heavens in the millennium, and the new
heaven and the new earth with the New Jerusalem as the consummation of the church and the kingdom. In each of these three
sections the kingdom of the Son of God's love is a matter of
delight. The Father, by His mercy and grace, has transferred us
out of the darkness of Satan into this pleasant part of the kingdom.

The stress in Colossians 1:13 is the kingdom of the Son of
God's love in this age, which is the reality of the church. (*The Conclusion of the New Testament,* p. 2583)

Today's Reading

If we are not born anew, we do not have the capacity to see the
kingdom of God [John 3:3]. To be born anew is to be born of water,

signifying the death of Christ, and of the Spirit, signifying Christ's resurrection [v. 5]. We need to die with Christ and be resurrected to be a new person of another, new species, new kind. The kingdom of God is the reign of God. This divine reign is a realm, not only of the divine dominion but also of the divine species, in which are all the divine things. The vegetable kingdom is a realm of the vegetable species, and the animal kingdom is a realm of the animal species. In the same way, the kingdom of God is a realm of the divine species.

God became flesh to enter into the human species, and man becomes God in His life and nature, but not in His divine Godhead, to enter into His divine species. In John 3 the kingdom of God refers more to the species of God than to the reign of God.... To enter into the divine realm, the realm of the divine species, we need to be born of God to have the divine nature and life.

Man was created in the image of God and after His likeness.... Genesis 1 says that each of the living things was created after its kind. But God created man, not after man's kind, but in God's image and after God's likeness to be God's kind.

The believers, who are born of God by regeneration to be His children in His life and nature but not in His Godhead (John 1:12-13), are more in God's kind than Adam was. Adam had only the outward appearance of God without the inward reality, the divine life. We have the reality of the divine life within us, and we are being transformed and conformed to the Lord's image in our entire being. It is logical to say that all the children of God are in the divine realm of the divine species.

If the children of God are not in God's kind, in God's species, in what kind are they?...We all who are born of God are gods. But for utterance, due to the theological misunderstanding, it is better to say that we are God-men in the divine species, that is, in the kingdom of God. (*Crystallization-study of the Gospel of John*, pp. 122-124)

Further Reading: Life-study of Colossians, msg. 4; *Crystallization-study of the Gospel of John,* msg. 12

Enlightenment and inspiration: _____

_____

_____

Morning Nourishment

Rev.   And made us a kingdom, priests to His God and
1:6   Father, to Him be the glory and the might forever and
ever. Amen.

Gal.   ...Those who practice such things will not inherit the
5:21, 25   kingdom of God....If we live by the Spirit, let us also
walk by the Spirit.

Today the believers live the kingdom life in the church, for the
church is the kingdom of God in this age (Matt. 16:18-19; 1 Cor.
6:10; Gal. 5:21; Eph. 5:5).

In the four Gospels the Lord Jesus mentioned the church twice,
both times in the Gospel of Matthew, a book that proclaims the
kingdom, [and] each time...in relation to the kingdom. This indicates how intimately the kingdom and the church are related.
(*The Conclusion of the New Testament*, pp. 1727, 1742)

Today's Reading

[Romans 14:17 says], "The kingdom of God is not eating and
drinking, but righteousness and peace and joy in the Holy Spirit."
According to some Bible teachers, the kingdom has not yet come.
...But...Paul does not say that the kingdom of God *shall be;* he
uses the present tense and says that the kingdom of God *is.*
According to the context of Romans 14, which speaks of receiving
the believers, the kingdom is today's church life. The reality of the
church life is the kingdom. (*The Conclusion of the New Testament*,
pp. 1727-1728)

[In 1 Corinthians 4:20 Paul says, "The kingdom of God is not in
speech but in power." Here *the kingdom of God*] refers to the
church life, implying that in the sense of authority the church in
this age is the kingdom of God. (1 Cor. 4:20, footnote 1)

In Colossians 4:11 the apostle Paul...[says] that his fellow
workers are the workers for the kingdom of God, indicating that
what they were doing in the gospel work for the establishing and
building up of the churches was for the kingdom of God today.
This means the kingdom of God is actually the reality of the
church today. (*The Conclusion of the New Testament*, p. 1729)

The believers redeemed by the blood of Christ have not only been born of God into His kingdom (John 3:5) but have also been made a kingdom for God's economy, which is the church ([Rev. 1:6]; Matt. 16:18-19). John, the writer of [Revelation], was in this kingdom (Rev. 1:9), and all the redeemed and reborn believers are a part of this kingdom (Rom. 14:17).

One of the main aspects of [the book of Revelation] is that God is recovering His right over the earth to make the whole earth His kingdom (Rev. 11:15). When Christ came, He brought in the kingdom of God with Him (Luke 17:21; Matt. 12:28). This kingdom has been enlarged into the church (Matt. 16:18-19), which will bring in the consummation of the kingdom of God to the whole earth. (*Life-study of Revelation,* p. 5)

The church revealed in Matthew 16:18 is the universal church, the unique Body of Christ, whereas the church revealed in Matthew 18:17 is the local church, the expression of the unique Body of Christ in a certain locality. Matthew 16 concerns the universal building of the church, but chapter eighteen concerns the local practice of the church. Both chapters indicate that the church represents the kingdom of the heavens, having the authority to bind and to loose.

Although the church today is God's kingdom, we are in the kingdom in reality only when we live and walk in spirit. Whenever we behave according to the old man or live in the flesh or the self, we, in a practical way, are out of God's kingdom. This means that when we are in the flesh, we are in the old realm of the fallen human nature, which has been fully usurped by Satan to form his kingdom. Therefore, a genuine Christian, if he lives in the flesh instead of in the spirit, may live in a practical way not in the kingdom of God but in the kingdom of Satan. Only when we live, walk, behave, and have our being altogether in our spirit, not in our natural man, are we in the kingdom of God and, in reality, are the kingdom of God. (*The Conclusion of the New Testament,* pp. 1754-1755, 2236)

Further Reading: The Conclusion of the New Testament, msgs. 159-161

Enlightenment and inspiration: _____

_____

_____

Morning Nourishment

2 Pet. For in this way the entrance into the eternal kingdom
1:11 of our Lord and Savior Jesus Christ will be richly *and*
bountifully supplied to you.
Matt. Your kingdom come; Your will be done, as in heaven,
6:10 *so* also on earth.

In Romans 14:17 we see that the kingdom of God is righteousness, peace, and joy in the Holy Spirit. When the authority of God's kingdom is allowed to operate in us, righteousness, peace, and joy will characterize our daily life. Righteousness, peace, and joy mean a great deal, for these items are the expression of Christ. When Christ is expressed, He is our righteousness toward ourselves, and our peace toward others, and our joy with God. (*The Conclusion of the New Testament*, p. 1728)

Today's Reading

After we have entered into the kingdom of God through regeneration, we need to go on to have a rich entrance into the eternal kingdom of our Lord and Savior Jesus Christ (2 Pet. 1:5-11). On the one hand, we have entered the kingdom; on the other hand, we still need a rich entrance. We may use the birth of a child into a family as an illustration....Birth is the initial entry into the family, but growth, development, and maturity produces a rich entry. The principle is the same with entering into the kingdom of God.

We have received the unique, eternal, common salvation (Titus 1:4), but we need to be faithful in taking the Lord's way in order to receive the reward of entering into His joy and of reigning with Him over the nations in the coming kingdom.

As those who are under the divine dispensing of the Divine Trinity, we need to live in the reality of the kingdom of the heavens today. We need to live a kingdom life in the church, developing ourselves in the divine life until we reach maturity. Then we shall have a rich entrance into the coming kingdom of our Lord and Savior Jesus Christ. Those who are faithful and reach maturity will receive a reward from the Lord, but those who are not faithful will suffer dispensational punishment. The incentive of the reward and the warning concerning punishment should encourage us to live in the reality of the kingdom of the heavens today, to be faithful in taking the Lord's way, and to be diligent to grow and mature in the divine life.

Eventually, if we live in the reality of the kingdom of the heavens and partake in the kingdom, we shall inherit the kingdom of God (1 Cor. 6:9a, 10b; Gal. 5:21b; Eph. 5:5b). Inheriting the kingdom of God is different from entering into the kingdom of God through regeneration. Having entered into the kingdom by being regenerated, we now need to grow and develop in the divine life. Then, as a result of this growth and development, we shall inherit the kingdom of God....We cannot inherit the kingdom unless we grow to maturity in the proper development in the divine life. (*The Conclusion of the New Testament,* pp. 1702-1703, 1737, 1732)

The work of the church on earth is to bring in the kingdom of God. All the work of the church is governed by the principle of the kingdom of God. The saving of souls is under this principle, and so is the casting out of demons and all other works as well. Everything should be under the principle of God's kingdom. Why should we win souls? For the sake of the kingdom of God—not just because man needs salvation. We must stand on the position of the kingdom of God whenever we work, and we must apply the kingdom of God to deal with the power of Satan. (Watchman Nee, *The Glorious Church,* p. 63)

The present age is the time for the church to practically realize the victory of Christ. The Head has overcome; now the Body must also overcome. The Lord destroyed the devil on the cross and produced the church with resurrection life. Today God is establishing His kingdom on earth through His church. The church must continue the victorious work that Christ has carried out against Satan. It is responsible for bringing heaven's will down to earth and for carrying it out on earth. (Watchman Nee, *God's Eternal Plan,* p. 54)

Further Reading: The Conclusion of the New Testament, msgs. 157-158; *God's Eternal Plan,* chs. 9-10

Enlightenment and inspiration: _____

_____

_____

Hymns, #941

1 God's kingdom is God's reigning,
   His glory to maintain;
   It is His sovereign ruling,
   His order to sustain.
   He exercises fully
   His own authority
   Within His kingdom ever
   And to eternity.

2 Upon the throne, the center
   Of government divine,
   God reigns, and with His purpose
   Brings everything in line.
   God's headship and His lordship
   He only can maintain
   As King within His kingdom,
   O'er everything to reign.

3 By reigning in His kingdom
   God worketh all His will,
   And under His dominion
   His purpose doth fulfill.
   'Tis only in God's kingdom
   His blessing we may know;
   'Tis from His throne almighty
   The stream of life doth flow.

4 Submitted to God's ruling,
   All virtue thus will win;
   Rebellion to His Headship
   Is but the root of sin.
   The evil aim of Satan—
   God's throne to overthrow;
   Our aim and goal is ever
   His rule to fully know.

5 Within God's sovereign kingdom
   His Christ is magnified;
   When Christ in life is reigning,
   The Father's glorified.
   When God is in dominion,
   All things are truly blessed;
   When Christ for God is reigning,
   God's glory is expressed.

6   In fulness of the seasons
      God's Christ will head up all,
    Then all will own His reigning
      And worship, great and small.
    Such reign in life and glory
      The Church e'en now foretastes,
    And to His rule submitting
      Unto His kingdom hastes.

Composition for prophecy with main point and sub-points: _____

_____

_____

_____

_____

_____

_____

_____

_____

_____

_____

_____

_____

_____

_____

_____

_____

_____

_____

_____

_____

_____

_____

_____

_____

_____

The Third Great Pillar—the Church
(2)
The Way to Build Up the Church
as the Kingdom of God—
Denying the Self, Taking Up the Cross,
and Losing the Soul-life

Scripture Reading: Matt. 16:16-28

Day 1
&
Day 2
I. **In Matthew 16 the way to build up the church**
   as the kingdom of God is revealed; the enemy
   of the building is also revealed (vv. 16-28):
   A. Christ, the Son of the living God, builds the church
      on Himself as the rock, with stones such as Peter, a
      transformed person (vv. 16-18).
   B. The gates of Hades, Satan's authority, or power of
      darkness, attacks the church to frustrate the Lord
      from building up the church (v. 18).
   C. In order to build the church, the Lord had to pass
      through death and enter into resurrection (v. 21):
      1. The church was produced through Christ's death
         and resurrection (John 12:24).
      2. The way to build the church is to be crucified
         and resurrected (cf. 2 Cor. 4:10-12; Gal. 2:20).
   D. Peter, with a good heart, rebuked the Lord and
      tried to prevent the Lord from going to Jerusalem
      to be crucified (Matt. 16:22):
      1. It was not Peter but Satan who came out
         through one of the gates of Hades, the gate of
         Peter's self, to try to frustrate the Lord from
         building up the church (v. 23).
      2. The self, the mind, and the soul-life are the
         main gates through which Satan comes forth
         to attack and damage the church (vv. 23-26).

Day 3
&
Day 4
II. **The building up of the church as the kingdom**
    of God depends on the shutting up of the gates
    of Hades through the exercise of three keys
    (vv. 24-26):

A. We need to learn to exercise the key of denying the
   self (v. 24):
   1. The self is the embodiment of Satan; the self is
      the soul plus the satanic mind, the mind of
      Satan (Gen. 3:1-6; Matt. 16:22-23):
      a. The self is the embodiment of the soul-life,
         which is expressed through the mind; thus,
         the self, the soul-life, and the mind are
         three-in-one.
      b. Behind these three is Satan, who manipu-
         lates the self in order to damage the church
         (v. 23).
   2. The self is the soul declaring independence
      from God:
      a. The Lord does not have regard for what we
         do; rather, He has regard for our dependence
         on Him (7:21-23).
      b. The enemy of the Body is the self; because
         the self is something independent, the self
         is the greatest problem, the greatest frus-
         tration and opposition, to the building up of
         the Body:
         (1) We should depend not only on God but
             also on the Body, on the brothers and
             sisters (Exo. 17:11-13; Acts 9:25; 2 Cor.
             11:33).
         (2) The Lord and the Body are one; hence,
             if we are dependent on the Body, we are
             also dependent on the Lord, and if we
             are independent of the Body, we are spon-
             taneously independent of the Lord.
         (3) When we are dependent, the self is gone,
             and instead of the self, we have the Lord's
             presence and are full of peace.
   3. When the self has been utterly dealt with by
      the cross, we are able to touch the reality of the
      Body of Christ and come to know the Body.
   4. We need to deny the following aspects of the self:
      a. Ambition, pride, and self-exaltation (Matt.

20:20-28; 1 Pet. 5:5; Rom. 12:3; Num. 12:1-10;
16:1-3; Phil. 2:3-4).

b. Self-righteousness, self-justification, and
exposing, criticizing, and condemning others
(Matt. 9:10-13; Luke 18:9-14; 1 Pet. 4:8; John
3:17; 8:11; Luke 6:37; Matt. 7:1-5).

c. Introspection and self-despising (S. S. 2:8-9;
1 Cor. 12:15-16).

d. Being offended by the church, the leading
ones, or the saints (Matt. 6:14-15; 18:21-35;
Mark 11:25-26; Col. 3:13).

e. Disappointment and discouragement (Rom.
8:28-29; 2 Cor. 4:1).

f. Self-love, self-preservation, self-seeking, and
self-pity (Matt. 13:5, 20-21).

g. Murmurings and reasonings (Exo. 16:1-9;
Phil. 2:14).

h. Natural affection (friendship) based on natural taste and preference (Matt. 12:46-50;
Phil. 2:2b; 1 Cor. 12:25).

i. Being opinionated and dissenting (John 11:21,
23-28, 39; Acts 15:35-39; cf. 1 Cor. 7:25, 40).

j. Being individualistic and independent (16:12).

5. We can deny the self by exercising our spirit to
know the indwelling Christ and the power of
His resurrection (Phil. 3:10; cf. S. S. 2:8-9, 14).

Day 5   B. We need to learn to exercise the key of taking up
the cross (Matt. 16:24):

1. To take up the cross simply means to take up
the will of God; the cross is God's will (cf. 26:39):

a. The Lord Jesus was willing to be crucified so
that through His death, His life might be
released to produce and build up the church
(John 12:24; 2 Cor. 4:12).

b. The Lord Jesus was willing to take up the cross
and be crucified for the fulfillment of God's will.

2. *Let him...take up his cross* (Matt. 16:24) means
that we are not forced to bear the cross but that
we willingly take it up.

3. The one church is God's will, and every brother and sister in the church is God's will; thus, to bear the cross is to bear the church and to bear all the saints so that we would have the genuine oneness (John 17:21-23; Eph. 4:3, 13; 1 Cor. 1:10; Phil. 2:2).

4. We need to remain on the cross by the power of the resurrected, pneumatic Christ in our spirit, keeping our old man under the termination of the cross day by day (Luke 14:27; Rom. 6:6; Gal. 2:20; Phil. 3:10; 1 Cor. 15:31).

Day 6   C. We need to learn to exercise the key of losing the soul-life (Matt. 16:25):

1. To save the soul-life is to please the self by allowing the soul to have its enjoyment; to lose the soul-life is to lose the enjoyment of the soul:

   a. Receiving God into man's spirit and expressing God through the soul should be man's joy and amusement (cf. Neh. 8:10; Rom. 14:17). 5 7p⁹

   b. The Lord Jesus lost the enjoyment of His soul in this age so that He might find His soul-life in the coming age (John 10:11; Isa. 53:12); we must do the same.

   c. If we save our soul-life in this age, we will lose it in the coming age, but if we lose our soul-life in this age, we will find it in the coming age (Matt. 16:25).

   d. We need to love the Lord Jesus and to hate and deny our soul-life, not loving our soul-life even unto death (1 Cor. 16:22; 2:9; Luke 14:26; 9:23; Rev. 12:11).

2. If we are willing to lose all our present soulish enjoyment for the Lord's sake, for the sake of the church, and for the sake of all the saints, others will be nourished by us and will be built up through us; this is not a suffering but a joy (Heb. 12:2).

3. The kingdom reward of sharing the King's joy in ruling over the earth in the manifestation of the kingdom depends upon whether or not we save our soul-life in this age or lose it (Matt. 16:25-28; 25:21, 23).

Morning Nourishment

Matt. And Simon Peter answered and said, You are the
16:16-18 Christ, the Son of the living God. And Jesus answered
and said to him, Blessed are you, Simon Barjona,
because flesh and blood has not revealed *this* to you,
but My Father who is in the heavens. And I also say to
you that you are Peter, and upon this rock I will build
My church, and the gates of Hades shall not prevail
against it.

This rock refers not only to Christ but also to this revelation
concerning Christ, a revelation that Peter received from the
Father. The church is built on Christ and on this revelation concerning Christ.
Gates of Hades refers to Satan's authority or power of darkness (Col. 1:13; Acts 26:18), which cannot prevail against the genuine church built by Christ upon this revelation concerning Him
as the rock, with stones such as Peter, a transformed human
being. This word of the Lord's indicates also that Satan's power of
darkness will attack the church. Hence, there is spiritual warfare
between Satan's power, which is his kingdom, and the church,
which is God's kingdom. (Matt. 16:18, footnotes 3, 6)

Today's Reading

In Matthew 16:18 the Lord Jesus said, "…You are Peter, and
upon this rock I will build My church, and the gates of Hades shall
not prevail against it." How can the church be built up in a practical way? The answer is found in verses 21 through 26. According
to biblical terms, the way to build up the church is to be crucified
and resurrected. Unless Christ had been crucified and resurrected, He could not build up the church. The church came into
existence through His death and resurrection. Verse 21 says,
"From that time Jesus began to show to His disciples that He
must go to Jerusalem and suffer many things from the elders and
chief priests and scribes and be killed and on the third day be
raised." This verse indicates that the way to build up the church is
through death and resurrection. On the mount the Lord Jesus

was transfigured. This transfiguration, however, was temporary. Through death and resurrection, Christ was permanently transfigured. Resurrection is a form of transfiguration. Through death and resurrection, Christ has entered into a realm of transfiguration. The church exists in this realm of transfiguration. It cannot exist in the natural life or with fleshly people. It can only exist in a realm of transfiguration. As long as we are in a natural realm or in a fleshly condition, we are through with the church.

[Hades] is a region where death prevails. After the Lord Jesus died, He took a tour of Hades. Acts 2:24 indicates that Hades tried its best to hold Him. However, because Christ is the resurrection, He could not be held by death. Death cannot overcome resurrection; on the contrary, resurrection always subdues death.

The gates are mentioned in Matthew 16:18 and the keys in verse 19. The enemy has the gates, but we have the keys. The gates do not overcome the keys, but the keys control the gates. The enemy's gates are much bigger than the keys, but the gates are nonetheless under the control of the keys, just as the doors of a building are controlled by the keys that open and close them. Hallelujah, we have the keys! Satan has many gates, but we have the keys.

Now we need to consider what the keys of the kingdom are. Shortly after I was saved, I was taught by a great Bible teacher that the keys of the kingdom given to Peter were two in number. Peter used the first key to open the gate for the Jewish believers to enter the kingdom of the heavens on the day of Pentecost (Acts 2:38-42); and he used the other to open the gate for the Gentile believers to enter the kingdom of the heavens in the house of Cornelius (Acts 10:34-48). I still believe that this teaching is correct. But, as we shall see, there is more to this matter of the keys than this. (*The Exercise of the Kingdom for the Building of the Church,* pp. 33-34, 23-24)

Further Reading: The Exercise of the Kingdom for the Building of the Church, ch. 3

Enlightenment and inspiration: _____

_____

_____

_____

Morning Nourishment

Matt. I will give to you the keys of the kingdom of the heav-
16:19 ens, and whatever you bind on the earth shall have
been bound in the heavens, and whatever you loose
on the earth shall have been loosed in the heavens.
21 From that time Jesus began to show to His disciples that He must go to Jerusalem and suffer
many things from the elders and chief priests and
scribes and be killed and on the third day be
raised.

In order to interpret the Bible, we must follow the basic
principle of taking care of the context of every verse. In Matthew 16, Christ, the Son of the living God, the church, the
kingdom, the gates of Hades, and the keys of the kingdom are
all revealed.

Matthew 16:22 says, "And Peter took Him aside and began
to rebuke Him, saying, *God* be merciful to You, Lord! This
shall by no means happen to You!" With a good heart, Peter
was telling the Lord that God should be merciful to Him. This
verse is difficult to translate. Some say it should be rendered,
"Lord, pity Yourself." According to this rendering, Peter was
telling the Lord to be merciful to Himself. Another translation
is, "God be merciful to You, Lord." It is difficult to determine
the subject, whether it is God or the Lord Jesus. At any rate,
the emphasis is on the self. Whether the subject is God or the
Lord Jesus, the self is emphasized. (*The Exercise of the Kingdom for the Building of the Church,* p. 24)

Today's Reading

Matthew 16:23 says, "But He turned and said to Peter, Get
behind Me, Satan!" Then in verses 24 and 25 the Lord said to
His disciples, "If anyone wants to come after Me, let him deny
himself and take up his cross and follow Me. For whoever
wants to save his soul-life shall lose it; but whoever loses his
soul-life for My sake shall find it." According to these verses,
the Lord is the pattern and the pathway. If anyone desires to

come after Him, that is, take Him as the pattern and the pathway, he must deny himself, take up his cross, and follow Him. Matthew 16:21 through 26 are necessary for the interpretation of verses 16 through 19. As we have seen, verse 18 speaks of the gates and verse 19 of the keys. In order to know what the gates and the keys are, we need to consider verses 21 through 26. Satan comes out through the gates. The first gate is the self. This means that we ourselves are one of the gates of Hades through which Satan comes out. Satan may come out through the gate of self even when we have a good heart. Whether our heart is good or evil, self is the first gate through which Satan comes out. In addition to the self, verses 21 through 26 also speak of the mind and the soul, both of which are also gates through which Satan comes out. Thus, the self, the soul, and the mind are the main gates through which Satan comes forth. Many times Satan has come out through your mind because your mind has been an open gate for him.

Verses 21 through 26 not only expose the gates but also reveal the keys. The first key is the denial of the self. Self is an open gate, but self-denial is the key that shuts it. The second key is the taking up of the cross. This means that the cross is a key to shut up the self, the soul, and the mind. The third key is the losing of the soul. Therefore, the three keys here are the denying of the self, the taking up of the cross, and the losing of the soul. Day by day we need to use these keys. Yes, Peter used the keys on the day of Pentecost and in the household of Cornelius. But we also need the three subjective keys found in this portion of the Word.

The principalities and powers in the heavenlies are gates. But in addition, the self, the soul, and the mind are three crucial subjective gates. If these subjective gates are locked, no principalities or powers will be able to come in. (*The Exercise of the Kingdom for the Building of the Church,* pp. 24-25)

Further Reading: Life-study of Matthew, msg. 48

Enlightenment and inspiration: _____

_____

_____

_____

Morning Nourishment

Matt. **But He turned and said to Peter, Get behind Me,**
16:23-24 **Satan! You are a stumbling block to Me, for you are**
not setting your mind on the things of God, but on the
things of men. Then Jesus said to His disciples, If
anyone wants to come after Me, let him deny himself
and take up his cross and follow Me.

My burden in this message is not interpretation; it is application. Throughout history, the church has not been damaged mainly
by Judaism or Gnosticism; it has been damaged mainly by the
self. Martin Luther once said that although he was afraid of the
pope, he was more afraid of the stronger pope, the self, within his
own heart. Nothing damages and frustrates the building up of the
church more than the self. Self is the embodiment of the soul,
which is expressed through the mind. Thus the self, the soul, and
the mind are three-in-one. Behind these three is Satan, who
manipulates the self in order to damage the church life. We all
need to heed this word for ourselves. (*The Exercise of the Kingdom*
for the Building of the Church, pp. 25-26)

Today's Reading

Let me honestly and lovingly say a word to you all: It is a very
serious matter to be offended....Although others may offend you,
you will always be the first to suffer. On the one hand, I condemn
all the offenses; but on the other hand, I must say that there is no
excuse for your being offended. If we were not in ourselves, we
could not be offended. If I exercise the key of self-denial to lock up
the self, it will be impossible for me to be offended. The reason we
are offended is that the self is so open and prevailing. Through the
open gate of the self, Satan comes forth, and we are offended.

Perhaps in certain matters the church may be wrong. Do not
think that the church is no longer the church because it is wrong.
...Whether the church is right or wrong, it is still the church.
Although you may be offended by something or someone in the
church, do not make any excuses for yourself. This frustrates the
building up of the church.

Matthew 16 speaks about the building up of the church and also about the gates of Hades and the keys of the kingdom. Without the keys to lock the gates, the church cannot be built. Because there has been so little exercise of these keys, the church has not yet been built. We may talk a great deal about the building. However, when certain things take place to touch us, the self is open. Because we are open to Hades, something from Hades—Satan—comes out. How we need to use the key of self-denial to lock the self! The way to keep from being offended by others is to lock up yourself by denying yourself. Blessed are those who are not offended. (*The Exercise of the Kingdom for the Building of the Church*, pp. 26-27)

The origin of the self was Satan's injecting his thought into the human mind....The self is the soul being independent of God. Whenever the soul is not dependent on God but is independent of Him, the soul immediately becomes the self....No matter what, ...as long as we are independent of God we are in the self.

If we have the vision of the self, we will see what the self is— the soul declaring its independence from God. If we see this vision, we will realize that we can no longer be independent of God. Then we will say, "I must depend on God all the time. Whatever I do, I must depend on God. Whatever I am, I must depend on God."

Because the self is something independent, the self is the greatest problem to the building up of the Body. We should be dependent not only on God but also on the Body, on the brothers and sisters. Whenever we are independent of the brothers and sisters, we are in the self, in the independent soul. For us today, being independent of the Body is equal to being independent of God. This is a matter not of doctrine but of experience. If you check with your experience, you will realize that when you were independent of the brothers and sisters, you had the sense that you were also independent of God. Likewise, when you were isolated from the brothers and sisters, you had the sense that you were also isolated from God. (*The Heavenly Vision*, pp. 43-44)

Further Reading: The Heavenly Vision, chs. 3-4

Enlightenment and inspiration: _____

_____

_____

_____

Morning Nourishment

Matt. **Not everyone who says to Me, Lord, Lord, will enter
7:21-23 into the kingdom of the heavens, but he who does the
will of My Father who is in the heavens. Many will
say to Me in that day, Lord, Lord, *was it* not in Your
name *that* we prophesied, and in Your name cast out
demons, and in Your name did many works of power?
And then I will declare to them: I never knew you.
Depart from Me, you workers of lawlessness.**

The self is the independent soul. In doing things, our motive,
intention, aim, and goal may all be right, but if we are independent, we are in the self. This may be our situation even in preaching the gospel, for we may preach the gospel in the self and by the
self. We may also do certain other works for the Lord, but we may
do them in the self and by the self.

[In Matthew 16:21-26] Peter was not doing something evil to
the Lord. On the contrary, he was acting out of love for Him and
intended to do something good for Him. Nevertheless, because
Peter was independent of the Lord, the Lord turned to Peter and
said, "Get behind Me, Satan!" This indicates that no matter what
we do, even if it is something very good, we are in the self whenever we are independent of the Lord.

From this we see that the Lord Jesus does not have regard for
what we do; rather, He has regard for our dependence on Him. If
we see this, we will pay attention not to what we do but to whether
or not we are dependent on the Lord....If we are independent of the
Lord, we are in the self. If we are dependent on the Lord, we are
spontaneously dependent on the Body. (*The Heavenly Vision*, p. 45)

Today's Reading

The Lord and the Body are one. If you are dependent on the
Lord, you are dependent on the Body. If you are dependent on
the Body, you are dependent on the Lord. If you are independent
of the Body, you are spontaneously independent of the Lord and
are in the self, no matter how many good things you intend to do.
...[And] because you are in the self, you are incorporated with Satan.

As long as we have no dependence on the Lord and on the Body, the self is here. But when we have dependence, the self is gone. Dependence brings peace. Actually, dependence is the real peace. How do we know that we are dependent on God? We know it by the genuine peace within us. When we are dependent on God, we are full of peace.

When we are dependent on the Lord and on the Body, there is no need for the self to manufacture a kind of peace and then strive to maintain this peace. A man-made peace is a peace which needs the self to sustain it. As soon as the self stops working at sustaining this kind of peace, the peace disappears. Genuine peace does not need to be sustained by the self. If you have a real dependence on the Lord and on the Body, automatically the peace will be there. You will know and others also will know that you are truly at peace.

Those who are independent of the Body not only do not have genuine peace within but also are exercised to talk with others in order to get the confirmation which they are seeking. Because they do not have peace, they expect others to tell them that they are right and to give them confirmation. They try to get confirmation in this way because they are not at peace. No one who is independent of the Body ever has real peace. Instead of peace, they have the self.

Seeing the vision of the self has much to do with the Body. Today we are in the Lord's recovery, and the recovery will eventually come to this crucial matter—the building up of the Body. The enemy of the Body is the self. The greatest problem, the greatest frustration and opposition, to the Body is also the self. When we have the self, we do not have the Body. When we have the Body, we do not have the self. In order for the Body to be built up, the self, the independent soul, must be dealt with. The self is the independent "I," the independent "me." When we are independent, we are in the self, the Body is gone, and we do not have peace. (*The Heavenly Vision*, pp. 45-47)

Further Reading: Basic Lessons on Service, lsn. 19

Enlightenment and inspiration: _____

_____

_____

Morning Nourishment

Matt. **Then Jesus said to His disciples, If anyone wants to**
16:24 **come after Me, let him...take up his cross and follow**
Me.

Phil. **To know Him and the power of His resurrection and**
3:10 **the fellowship of His sufferings, being conformed to**
His death.

We need to know the genuine meaning of the cross. Yes, the
cross is a matter of suffering.... [However, the Lord Jesus] was not
forced to suffer crucifixion; He chose it. This was His own preference. He was not compelled to go to the cross; He was willing to do
so because His cross was God's will. Hence, His crucifixion was for
the fulfillment of God's will. The Lord was willing to take up the
cross and be crucified for the fulfillment of God's purpose. In other
words, Christ was not forced to die like a criminal. Rather, He
was willing to be crucified that through death His life might be
released to produce the church. (*The Exercise of the Kingdom for
the Building of the Church,* p. 35)

Today's Reading

According to [the] principle of first mention, all the other crosses
must be the same as the first cross. This means that we are not
forced to bear the cross, but that we willingly take it up. Notice,
the Lord Jesus did not say, "Let him deny himself and be crucified." No, He said, "Let him take up his cross." We are not to be crucified, but we are to pick up the cross. However, certain brothers
have said, "I have been crucified by my dear wife many times."
Such brothers are not cross-bearers; they are criminals executed
by their wives.

The Lord did not suffer as a criminal, but...He willingly took
up His cross. He was a willing and happy cross-bearer for the purpose of fulfilling God's will to produce the church. Through His
death, His divine life was released to us, making us the members
of the church. Today the problem is not with Him; it is with us.
Although we have the divine life within us and have become
members of the church, the problem is whether or not we shall be

built up. We all have the divine life in us for the church, but we have not yet been built together. To take up the cross simply means to take up God's will. The cross is actually God's will. Anything that is not God's will is not a cross. The cross experienced by Christ definitely was God's will. We may apply the same principle to the church life. In the universe there is just one church, and in any locality there should also be one church. The one church is God's ordination and allotment. This is His portion to us, and this is His will. Whether we like the church or not does not mean anything, because the church is God's will. Perhaps at first you were very happy with the church, ...but later you came to dislike the church and desired a separation from it....Therefore, eventually the church becomes the cross that we must bear. The question is whether we shall bear it like a criminal being executed or bear it willingly and happily. We should be like Christ who made the cross His choice, His first preference....[Then we] will become a happy bearer of the cross, not a criminal. As a result, you will have the genuine building.

Not only is the church God's will, but every brother and sister in the church is also His will. According to the Bible, we have no way to divide ourselves from the brothers and sisters....The Father has begotten them all, and we need to accept them all as His will. There is no room for our likes or dislikes, both of which are natural. In the church there are no special friendships and no preferences. Thus, eventually every brother and sister becomes a cross to us.

Thus, you must use the second key—the taking up of the cross. We need to say, "Lord, Your will is that there be one church in the universe and one church in every city. Lord, Your will is also that I be one with all my brothers and sisters. As long as anyone is a believer, I must accept him....My likes or dislikes do not mean anything." This is the unique way for us to be built together. (*The Exercise of the Kingdom for the Building of the Church,* pp. 36-40)

Further Reading: The Exercise of the Kingdom for the Building of the Church, ch. 4

Enlightenment and inspiration: _____

_____

_____

_____

Morning Nourishment

Matt.   For whoever wants to save his soul-life shall lose it;
16:25-26   but whoever loses his soul-life for My sake shall find
it. For what shall a man be profited if he gains the
whole world, but forfeits his soul-life? Or what shall a
man give in exchange for his soul-life?

Luke   For what is a man profited if he gains the whole world
9:25   but loses or forfeits himself?

God's intention in His creation of man was that man would
take Him in and express Him. Taking in God and expressing God
should be man's joy and amusement. Man's happiness and enter-
tainment must be God Himself, and this is not an objective God,
but a subjective God. To take God in and to live God out is man's joy.
(*The Exercise of the Kingdom for the Building of the Church*, p. 58)

Today's Reading

In Matthew 16:25 the word *soul-life* indicates enjoyment. If
you consider the context of verses 25 through 27, you will see that
the Lord is speaking about the enjoyment of the soul....To lose the
soul-life means to lose the enjoyment of the soul, and to gain the
soul-life means to have the enjoyment of the soul [cf. Luke 9:25].

This reward, however, is not strictly a matter of the future.
This is proved by verse 28: "Truly I say to you, There are some of
those standing here who shall by no means taste death until they
see the Son of Man coming in His kingdom." The Lord will come
in two ways, in His coming in the future and in His coming in His
transfiguration. The Lord's transfiguration on the mountain was
a form of the coming of the kingdom. In both types of comings
there is a reward according to our doings, according to whether or
not we deny ourselves, take up the cross, and lose the soul.

The subject of the last half of Matthew 16 is the building of the
church, and...we should not isolate verses 21 through 28 from
verses 16 through 19 since these verses are concerned with the
way to build up the church.

In the process of the building of the church, we should not save
our soul-life. Rather, we must always lose it....[This is] the third

key, the key of losing the soul-life.

The Lord's interest today is with the building of the church. But how can we, as fallen human beings, be built up together? It is difficult even for a husband and wife or for parents and children to be built up together. We all want enjoyment for ourselves and react against anything that touches our sense of enjoyment. Apart from the losing of the soul-life, it is impossible for the church to be built up. If someone offends you, you may be unwilling to forgive him simply because you enjoy being able to condemn him. Because forgiving him is not enjoyable to you, you have no interest in forgiving him....This is the saving of the soul-life....If you are willing to lose your soulish enjoyment, you will be rewarded one day when the Lord comes into your [situation]....At that time, the Lord will save your soul. You were willing to lose it, but when the Lord comes in, He will save it and cause you to have great enjoyment. For the building of the church there is the crucial need that we all learn to lose our soul. Do not keep any enjoyment for your soul. Rather, lose it for the Lord's sake.

The losing of the soul-life is the basic factor in our being built up together....We need to lose all our present soulish enjoyment for the Lord's sake, for the sake of the church, and for the sake of all the saints. If you are willing to lose your soul for the sake of others, those with you will be enlightened, nourished, and filled. This is the way the church is built. If all the saints are willing to lose the soul, what a wonderful situation there will be among us. There will be no offenses and even no need for forgiveness. If we are like this, we shall be rewarded with a prevailing transfiguration....Our willingness to lose the soul for the Lord's sake will cause the church to be transfigured. In other words, it will bring in a revival. Every genuine revival is a coming of Christ, a present coming of Christ with His reward (not His second coming in a physical way). (*The Exercise of the Kingdom for the Building of the Church,* pp. 44-49)

Further Reading: The Exercise of the Kingdom for the Building of the Church, chs. 5-6

Enlightenment and inspiration: _____

_____

_____

_____

Hymns, #840

1　Freed from self and Adam's nature,
　　Lord, I would be built by Thee
　With the saints into Thy temple,
　　Where Thy glory we shall see.
　From peculiar traits deliver,
　　From my independent ways,
　That a dwelling place for Thee, Lord,
　　We will be thru all our days.

2　By Thy life and by its flowing
　　I can grow and be transformed,
　With the saints coordinated,
　　Builded up, to Thee conformed;
　Keep the order in the Body,
　　There to function in Thy will,
　Ever serving, helping others,
　　All Thy purpose to fulfill.

3　In my knowledge and experience
　　I would not exalted be,
　But submitting and accepting
　　Let the Body balance me;
　Holding fast the Head, and growing
　　With His increase, in His way,
　By the joints and bands supplying,
　　Knit together day by day.

4　By Thy Spirit daily strengthened
　　In the inner man with might,
　I would know Thy love surpassing,
　　Know Thy breadth and length and height;
　Ever of Thy riches taking,
　　Unto all Thy fulness filled,
　Ever growing into manhood,
　　That Thy Body Thou may build.

5　In God's house and in Thy Body
　　Builded up I long to be,
　That within this corporate vessel
　　All shall then Thy glory see;
　That Thy Bride, the glorious city,
　　May appear upon the earth,
　As a lampstand brightly beaming
　　To express to all Thy worth.

*Composition for prophecy with main point and
sub-points:* _____

_____
_____
_____
_____
_____
_____
_____
_____
_____
_____
_____
_____
_____
_____
_____
_____
_____
_____
_____
_____
_____
_____
_____
_____
_____
_____
_____
_____
_____
_____
_____

The Fourth Great Pillar—the Gospel (1)
Blood and Water

Scripture Reading: John 19:34, 36; Gen. 2:21-24

Day 1   I. Our hymns are full of precious truths that en-
able us to preach the high gospel to people; for
example, the first stanza of *Hymns,* #1058 says,
"Rock of Ages, cleft for me, / Let me hide myself
in Thee; / Let the water and the blood, / From
Thy riven side which flowed, / Be of sin the double
cure, / Save me from its guilt and power":
   A. We need to take note of *the water and the blood, the
double cure,* and *guilt and power.*
   B. The *double cure* refers to the cure of our outward
sinful acts by the Lord's precious blood to save us
from the guilt of sin, and it refers to the cure of our
inward sinful nature by the Lord's flowing life to
save us from the power of sin.
   C. The blood refers to the precious blood shed by the
Lord to deal with our outward sinful acts (John
1:29; Heb. 9:22), and the water refers to the life
imparted by the Lord to deal with our inward
sinful nature (John 19:34).
   D. The precious blood of the Lord redeems us from the
eternal punishment that we deserve due to our
sinful acts, and His life saves us from the power of
our sinful nature.
   E. If we have a thorough understanding of the stanza
of this hymn, we will be able to preach the high
gospel to people, because this "double cure" of blood
and water fulfills God's original intention with man.

Day 2 II. Two substances came out of the Lord's pierced
side: blood and water (v. 34):
   A. We sinners became fallen and were then against
God's righteousness and estranged from God's life
(Gen. 3:24; Eph. 4:18).

B. As sinners, we need to be redeemed judicially from God's condemnation according to the righteous requirement of His law (Gal. 3:13), and we need to be saved organically by His life from the death brought in by sin (2 Tim. 1:10; Rom. 5:10, 12, 17, 21).

C. God's full salvation for us is judicial according to His righteousness and organic according to His life.

D. Christ, as the Redeemer and Savior of fallen man, redeems us and saves us through His death and resurrection.

E. In His crucifixion, after He was pierced by a soldier, blood and water, two elements which are critical to human life, came out of Him (John 19:34):

   1. Blood is for God's judicial redemption to deal with sins (1:29; Heb. 9:22) for the purchasing of the church (Acts 20:28):

      a. Redeeming the believers (Eph. 1:7; 1 Pet. 1:18-19; Gal. 3:13; 4:5).

      b. Forgiving the believers' sins (Heb. 9:22).

      c. Washing away the believers' sins (1:3).

      d. For God to justify the believers (Rom. 3:24; 5:9).

      e. Sanctifying the believers positionally (Heb. 13:12; 10:29).

      f. Speaking something better for the New Testament believers before God (12:24).

      g. Overcoming Satan, the accuser of the believers (Rev. 12:11).

      h. Thus, it is the precious blood of Christ (1 Pet. 1:19).

      i. It is also considered God's own blood, which is very dear to God and with which God has purchased and obtained the church as His flock (Acts 20:28).

   2. Water, signifying the divine life, is for God's organic salvation—for imparting life (John 12:24; 3:14-15) for the producing and building up of the church (Eph. 5:29-30):

    a. The Lord promises to give the sinners the water of life (John 4:10, 14; Rev. 21:6).

    b. The Lord calls the sinners to come and drink His water of life (22:17; John 7:37-38):

      (1) The believers are regenerated by God with His divine life (1 Pet. 1:3).

      (2) The divine life saves the believers (Rom. 5:10b).

      (3) The divine life dispositionally sanctifies (6:19, 22), renews (12:2b; Titus 3:5), transforms (Rom. 12:2a; 2 Cor. 3:18), conforms (Rom. 8:29), and glorifies (v. 30) the believers.

      (4) The believers reign in life (5:17).

      (5) The believers grow in life for the building up of the Body of Christ (Eph. 4:15-16).

      (6) The divine life consummates the New Jerusalem, which is wholly supplied with the river of water of life and with the tree of life (Rev. 21:2; 22:1-2).

Day 3
&
Day 4

III. **The flowing water and the unbroken bone mentioned by John in 19:34 and 36 are signs that relate to the life-releasing aspect of His death and the life-imparting aspect of His resurrection for the producing of His bride, His counterpart (Gen. 2:21-24):**

  A. In order to produce a complement for Himself, God first became a man (John 1:14), as typified by God's creation of Adam (Rom. 5:14).

  B. Adam's deep sleep for the producing of Eve as his wife typifies Christ's death on the cross (1 Cor. 15:18; 1 Thes. 4:13-16; John 11:11-14) for the producing of the church as His complement (Gen. 2:21; Eph. 5:25-27).

  C. Through Christ's death, the divine life within Him was released, and through His resurrection, His released divine life was imparted into His believers for the constituting of the church.

  D. Through such a process, God in Christ has been

wrought into man with His life and nature so that man can be the same as God in life and nature in order to match Him as His counterpart.

Day 5
E. The rib taken from Adam's opened side (Gen. 2:21) typifies the unbreakable, indestructible eternal life of Christ (Heb. 7:16; John 19:36), which flowed out of His pierced side (v. 34) to impart life to His believers for the producing and building up of the church as His complement:

1. When Adam was created, there was no sin, so there was no need of redemption; it was not until Genesis 3 that sin came in.

2. Thus, all that came out of Adam's side was the rib, without the blood.

3. However, by the time that Christ was sleeping on the cross, there was the problem of sin; thus, His death had to deal with the sin problem.

4. The blood came out of Christ's side for judicial redemption; following the blood, the water came out, which is the flowing life to produce and build up the church.

5. This divine, flowing, uncreated life is typified by the rib taken out of Adam's side.

Day 6
6. "These things happened that the Scripture might be fulfilled: 'No bone of His shall be broken'" (John 19:36):

   a. In the Scriptures the first mention of a bone is in Genesis 2:21-23; there it was a rib taken out of Adam for the producing and building of Eve as a match for Adam.

   b. Eve is a type of the church, which is produced and built with the Lord's resurrection life released out of Him.

   c. Hence, the bone is a symbol, a figure, of the Lord's resurrection life, which nothing can break.

   d. The Lord's side was pierced, but not one of His bones was broken; this signifies that although the Lord's physical life was terminated, His resurrection life, the very divine life, could not be hurt or damaged by anything.

e. This is the life with which the church is produced and built; it is also the eternal life, which we have obtained by believing into Him (John 3:36).

7. The building of Eve with the rib taken from Adam's side typifies the building of the church with the resurrection life released from Christ through His death on the cross and imparted into His believers in His resurrection (Gen. 2:22-24; John 12:24; 1 Pet. 1:3).

8. The church as the real Eve is the totality of Christ in all His believers; only that which comes out of Christ, having His resurrection life, can be His complement and counterpart, the Body of Christ (1 Cor. 12:12; Eph. 5:28-30).

9. Day by day as we enjoy this flowing, divine, uncreated, unbreakable, resurrection life, we are being transformed, and as we are being transformed, we are also being built into the church to be the bride to match Christ as His counterpart (Matt. 16:18).

10. At the end of Genesis 2 there is Eve, and at the end of the entire Bible there is the New Jerusalem, which is the ultimate Eve, the ultimate consummation of the eternal bride built up with precious materials produced by the flowing, resurrection life of Christ.

11. May we all be brought into the enjoyment and experience of this flowing, transforming, and building life to be prepared as the bride of Christ that will bring Christ back.

Morning Nourishment

John 1:29	**...Behold, the Lamb of God, who takes away the sin of the world!**
Heb. 9:22	**And almost all things are purified by blood according to the law, and without shedding of blood there is no forgiveness.**
John 19:34	**But one of the soldiers pierced His side with a spear, and immediately there came out blood and water.**

We all have the heart to preach the gospel, but if we do not know the truth, we will quickly run out of words as soon as we open our mouths to speak to people. After two or three sentences we will not know what to say,...and people will be unwilling to listen to us. Hence, we must learn the truth. The word of the gospel is the truth. For us to speak the word of the truth, we must first learn the truth. If from now on we would be willing to seriously learn the truth, we all would know how to preach the gospel in two months....The real gospel preaching is the speaking of the truth. To speak the truth is to preach the gospel; thus, we all must learn the truth in a proper way. (*Truth, Life, the Church, and the Gospel—the Four Great Pillars in the Lord's Recovery*, p. 126)

Today's Reading

Today the truth is needed everywhere. Not only the non-Christians do not know the truth; even many Christians do not know the truth. However, the Lord has given us many rich truths. Even our gospel hymns are full of precious truths. For example, the first stanza of *Hymns*, #1058 says, "Rock of Ages, cleft for me, / Let me hide myself in Thee; / Let the water and the blood, / From Thy riven side which flowed, / Be of sin the double cure, / Save me from its guilt and power." Here it mentions *the water and the blood, the double cure,* and *guilt and power.* Even many saints among us may not know the meanings of these phrases. Here the double cure refers to the cure of our outward sinful acts and our inward sinful nature. The blood refers to the precious blood shed by the Lord to deal with our outward sinful acts (John 1:29; Heb. 9:22), and the water refers to the life imparted by the Lord to deal with our inward sinful nature (John 19:34). The precious blood of the Lord redeems us from the eternal punishment we deserve due to our sinful acts, and His life saves us from the power of our sinful nature.

If we have a thorough understanding of this hymn, we will be able to preach the high gospel to people. We may invite someone to sing this hymn with us and then explain it to him. This would be a very good gospel message. After hearing this, he will be surprised and will respect the excellence and mysteriousness of the content of the gospel. When we speak to him, the Holy Spirit will work in him. Then we could sing this hymn with him again. In this way, he would probably be saved in less than half an hour. We should not say anything about perdition and "heaven" or even prosperity and peace. Instead, we should speak only about Christ Jesus, the Rock of Ages, who was crucified for us, and out from whose riven side came blood for redeeming us from the eternal punishment that we deserved due to our sins, and water for saving us out of the power of sin. This kind of simple but excellent singing and speaking, matched by the working of the Holy Spirit, will lead people to salvation. This is the proper way to preach the gospel today.

First Timothy 3:15b says, "The church...the pillar and base of the truth." This indicates that without the truth, there would be no church. The truth brings in life, and once we have life, we become the church. In addition, the unique commission of the church today is to preach the gospel, the content of which is the truth. The truth tells us one central point: the Triune God—the Father, the Son, and the Spirit—is dispensing Himself into us—sinful, tripartite men—that our sins may be forgiven and that we may receive God's life and have God Himself in us for our transformation into the sons of God. This is the truth and the gospel. We must learn the truth. (*Truth, Life, the Church, and the Gospel— the Four Great Pillars in the Lord's Recovery,* pp. 126-127)

Further Reading: Truth, Life, the Church, and the Gospel—the Four Great Pillars in the Lord's Recovery, ch. 10; The Organic Aspect of God's Salvation, chs. 1-2, 5

Enlightenment and inspiration: _____

_____

_____

Morning Nourishment

Eph. **Being darkened in their understanding, alienated**
4:18 **from the life of God...**
Rev. **And he showed me a river of water of life, bright as**
22:1-2 **crystal, proceeding out of the throne of God and of the**
Lamb in the middle of its street. And on this side and
on that side of the river was the tree of life...

God closed the way to the tree of life by means of three items:
the cherubim, the flame, and the sword [Gen. 3:24]. Cherubim
signify God's glory (cf. Ezek. 9:3; 10:4; Heb. 9:5), the flame signifies
God's holiness (Deut. 4:24; 9:3; Heb. 12:29), and the sword for kill-
ing indicates God's righteousness (cf. Lam. 3:42-43; Rom. 2:5).
These attributes of God placed requirements on sinful man. Since
sinful man was unable to meet these requirements (Rom. 3:10-18,
23), he was not permitted to contact God as the tree of life, until
Christ fulfilled the requirements of God's glory, holiness, and
righteousness by His all-inclusive death on the cross to open a
new and living way for us to enter the Holy of Holies and partake
of the tree of life. (Gen. 3:24, footnote 1)

We sinners became fallen and were then against God's righteousness and estranged from God's life (Gen. 3:24; Eph. 4:18).

As sinners, we need to be redeemed judicially from God's condemnation according to the righteous requirement of His law
(Gal. 3:13) and to be saved organically by His life from the death
brought in by sin (2 Tim. 1:10; Rom. 5:10, 12, 17, 21). (*Crystallization-study of the Gospel of John*, p. 124)

Today's Reading

God's full salvation for us is judicial according to His righteousness and organic through His life....Christ, as the Redeemer
and Savior of fallen man, redeems and saves us through His
death and resurrection....In His crucifixion, after He was pierced
by a soldier, blood and water, two elements which are critical to
human life, came out of Him (John 19:34).

The blood of Christ is for God's judicial redemption in His redeeming the believers (Eph. 1:7; 1 Pet. 1:18-19), forgiving the believers'

sins (Heb. 9:22), and washing away the believers' sins (Heb. 1:3). The blood of Christ is also for God to justify the believers (Rom. 3:24; 5:9) and sanctify the believers positionally (Heb. 13:12; 10:29). This blood speaks something better for the New Testament believers before God (Heb. 12:24). By the blood of Christ, the Lamb, we can overcome Satan, the accuser of the believers (Rev. 12:11). Thus, it is the precious blood of Christ (1 Pet. 1:19).

Acts 20:28 says that God...[obtained] the church with His own blood. If He were merely God, He could not have blood. God's own blood is the blood of the man Jesus Christ, who is the very God. God's purchasing the church with His own blood indicates the preciousness, the exceeding worth, of the church in the eyes of God. The church is dear to God, so we have to regard and respect the church.

Water, signifying the divine life,...is for God's organic salvation. The Lord promises to give the sinners the water of life (John 4:10, 14; Rev. 21:6).

Also, the Lord calls the sinners to come and drink His water of life (Rev. 22:17; John 7:37-38). The believers were regenerated by God with His divine life (1 Pet. 1:3). This divine life saves the believers (Rom. 5:10b). It dispositionally sanctifies (Rom. 6:19, 22), renews (Rom. 12:2b; Titus 3:5), transforms (Rom. 12:2; 2 Cor. 3:18), conforms (Rom. 8:29), and glorifies (Rom. 8:30) the believers. The believers reign in it (Rom. 5:17). We can be kings by this divine life. The believers also grow with it for the building up of the Body of Christ (Eph. 4:15-16). We all have to grow into the Head, Christ. Then out from Him we have something of the divine life to minister to the Body for its building up. This consummates the New Jerusalem, which is wholly supplied with the river of water of life and with the tree of life (Rev. 21:2; 22:1-2). The river of water of life signifies the Spirit of life, and the tree of life signifies Christ as the embodiment of the divine life. Both are for the supply of the New Jerusalem. (*Crystallization-study of the Gospel of John*, pp. 125-126)

Further Reading: Crystallization-study of the Gospel of John, msg. 12;
The Normal Christian Life, ch. 1

Enlightenment and inspiration: _____

_____

_____

_____

Morning Nourishment

Gen. And Jehovah God caused a deep sleep to fall upon the
2:21-23 man, and he slept; and He took one of his ribs and
closed up the flesh in its place. And Jehovah God built
the rib, which He had taken from the man, into a
woman and brought her to the man. And the man
said, This time this is bone of my bones and flesh of
my flesh; this one shall be called Woman because out
of Man this one was taken.

In Genesis 2 there is the picture of how the bride of Christ
comes into being. Before God prepared a bride for Adam, He
brought all the beasts and animals to Adam, and Adam named
each one. But none of these created things matched Adam, and
they could not be his counterpart (vv. 19-20). Then God caused a
deep sleep to fall upon Adam (v. 21). Adam is a type of Christ
(Rom. 5:14), and his sleep is a type of Christ's death.

During Adam's sleep, God took one of his ribs from his side.
Likewise, when Christ was sleeping on the cross, something came
out of His side,...blood and water [John 19:34]. At Adam's time
there was no sin, so there was no need of redemption. It was not
until Genesis 3 that sin came in. Thus, all that came out of Adam's
side was the rib without the blood. However, by the time that
Christ was sleeping on the cross, there was the problem of sin.
Thus,...the blood came out of Christ's side for redemption. Following the blood the water came out, which is the flowing life to
produce the church. This divine, flowing, uncreated life is typified
by the rib taken out of Adam's side. (*The Crucial Revelation of Life
in the Scriptures,* p. 20)

Today's Reading

When the Lord Jesus was dying on the cross, two others were
dying with Him. Their legs were broken, but when the soldier
came to the Lord Jesus, He was already dead and there was
no need to break His bones. This fulfilled the prophecy that not
one of His bones would be broken (John 19:31-33). Thus, the
bone taken out of Adam's side signifies the Lord's unbroken,

unbreakable, resurrection life. His resurrection life is unbreakable. The rib taken out of Adam signifies the resurrection life, and God built a woman with the rib of Adam. Now God builds up the church with the resurrection life of Christ. Just as Eve was a part of Adam, so the church is a part of Christ. Eve was bone of Adam's bones and flesh of Adam's flesh. Today we as the church are a part of Christ (Eph. 5:30-32). This marvelous revelation can be seen by comparing Genesis 2, John 19, and Ephesians 5.

When we received the Lord Jesus, He came into us as the resurrection life, the unbreakable life. It is this life that transforms us. This life is the tree of life, the river of life, the very life that supplies us and that flows within us to transform us. Day by day as we enjoy this flowing, divine, uncreated, unbreakable life, we are being transformed [Rom. 12:2; 2 Cor. 3:18]....As we are being transformed, we are also being built into the church to be the bride to satisfy Christ as His counterpart. At the end of Genesis 2 is Eve, and at the end of the entire Bible is the New Jerusalem, which is the ultimate Eve, the ultimate consummation of the universal bride built up with precious materials produced by the resurrection life of Christ.

The life seen in Genesis 2 is the flowing life, the transforming life, and the building life. This life flows within us, transforms us, and eventually builds us up as the bride of Christ. This bride, the New Jerusalem, will fulfill the two aspects of the purpose of God. First, the New Jerusalem will be the full expression of God in God's full image (Rev. 21:11; cf. 4:3). Second, this New Jerusalem will subdue the enemy, conquer the earth, and exercise God's authority over the entire universe, especially over the creeping things (Rev. 22:5; 21:15; cf. 21:8; 20:10, 14-15)....May we all be brought into the enjoyment and experience of this flowing, transforming, and building life to be prepared as the bride that will bring Christ back. (*The Crucial Revelation of Life in the Scriptures*, pp. 20-21)

Further Reading: The Crucial Revelation of Life in the Scriptures, ch. 2

Enlightenment and inspiration: _____

_____

_____

Morning Nourishment

Num.   They shall not leave any of it until the morning, nor
9:12   break a bone of it...
John   For these things happened that the Scripture might
19:36 be fulfilled: "No bone of His shall be broken."
Heb.   Who has been appointed not according to the law of a
7:16   fleshy commandment but according to the power of
       an indestructible life.

What did God do in order to produce a complement for Himself?...One day God became a man (John 1:14). This man was born of a virgin in the town of Bethlehem and was named Jesus. God becoming man was typified by the creation of man. Before creation there was no man. By God's sovereign creation a man suddenly came into being. Likewise, before the birth of Jesus in the manger at Bethlehem, God was only God. However, through the incarnation God became a man. This man was the real Adam. The Adam in Genesis 2 was a photograph (Rom. 5:14); with the birth of Christ in the flesh, the real Adam came. According to the Bible, Adam in the garden is called the first Adam, and the Lord Jesus as the real Adam is called the last Adam (1 Cor. 15:45). As the last One He is the real One. (*Life-study of Genesis*, p. 218)

Today's Reading

One day the real Adam was put to sleep on the cross...."God caused a deep sleep to fall upon the man" and..."He took one of his ribs" to build him a wife (Gen. 2:21[-22]). That sleep of Adam's was a type of Christ's death on the cross for producing the church. This is the life-releasing, life-imparting, life-propagating, life-multiplying, and life-reproducing death of Christ, which is signified by a grain of wheat falling into the ground to die and to grow up in order to produce many grains (John 12:24) for the making of the loaf which is the Body, the church (1 Cor. 10:17). By producing the church in this way God in Christ has been wrought into man as life. Firstly, God became a man. Then this man with the divine life and nature was multiplied through death and resurrection into many believers who become the many members to compose the real Eve to match Him and to complement Him. It is through this process that God in Christ has been wrought into man with His life and nature that man in life and nature can be the same as He is in order to match Him as His complement.

When the soldiers came to Jesus to break His legs, they found that He had died already and that there was no need for them to break His bones. This fulfilled the scripture which said, "No bone of His shall be broken" (John 19:32-33, 36; Exo. 12:46; Num. 9:12; Psa. 34:20). Nevertheless, the soldiers pierced His side and blood and water came out (John 19:34). The blood was for redemption (Heb. 9:22; 1 Pet. 1:18-19). What does the water signify? In Exodus 17:6 we find the type of the smitten rock (1 Cor. 10:4). After the rock was smitten, it was cleft, and living water came forth. Jesus on the cross was smitten with the rod of Moses, that is, by the law of God. He was cleft. His side was pierced, and water came forth. This water was the flow of His divine life signifying the life which produces the church.

This life was typified by the rib, a piece of bone taken out of Adam's opened side, of which Eve was produced and built. Hence, the bone typifies the divine life that is signified by the water flowing out of Christ's side. None of His bones was broken. This signifies that His divine life cannot be broken. His physical life was killed, but nothing could break His divine life which flows out to produce the church.

After God finished the work of producing Eve during Adam's sleep, Adam awoke from his sleep. As Adam's sleep typifies the death of Christ, so his waking signifies the resurrection of Christ. After waking, Adam became another person with Eve produced out of him. After His resurrection Christ also became another person with the church brought forth out of Him. As Adam eventually awoke from his sleep to take Eve as his counterpart, so Christ was also resurrected from the dead to take the church as His complement. (*Life-study of Genesis,* pp. 219-220)

Further Reading: Life-study of Genesis, msg. 17

Enlightenment and inspiration: _____

_____

_____

_____

Morning Nourishment

Eph. **Husbands, love your wives even as Christ also loved**
5:25-27 **the church and gave Himself up for her that He**
might sanctify her, cleansing *her* **by the washing of**
the water in the word, that He might present the
church to Himself glorious, not having spot or wrin-
kle or any such things, but that she would be holy
and without blemish.

When Adam awoke from his sleep, he immediately discovered
that Eve, who was builded with His rib, was present. Likewise,
when Christ was resurrected from the dead (1 Cor. 15:20), the
church was brought forth with His divine life. Through His death
the divine life within Him was released, and through His resurrection this released, divine life was imparted into us who believe
in Him. So, the Bible says that through His resurrection we were
regenerated (1 Pet. 1:3). He was the grain of wheat that fell into
the ground and died and produced many grains (John 12:24). We
are the many grains who have been regenerated with His resurrection life. As regenerated ones who have Him as life and who
live by Him, we compose His church, the real Eve in resurrection.

When Adam saw Eve he said, "This time this is bone of my
bones and flesh of my flesh" (Gen. 2:23, Heb.). When Christ saw
the church He might have said, "...This time this is bone of My
bones and flesh of My flesh, for the church is produced by My
death and resurrection. The church comes out of Me. The church
and I can be one." (*Life-study of Genesis,* pp. 220-221)

Today's Reading

After seeing the significance of the type of Adam and Eve in
Genesis 2, we can never again refer to a physical building as the
church....[Some may] say that the church is a group of genuine
Christians. However, a group of genuine Christians may not constitute the church. They may still be the natural man, so many
Americans, Chinese, Japanese, and Mexicans. Such a gathering
of the natural man is not the church.

What is the church? The church is a part of Christ; it is nothing less than Christ Himself. The church is the element of Christ in the believers. When this element in so many believers is added together, it equals the church....The church is the totality of the Christ in all His believers. Although we are regenerated people, if we live and act according to our natural disposition, we are not in reality members of the Body of Christ....What actually is a member of Christ? It is a person produced with the element of Christ, who is the life-giving Spirit in our spirit....When this Christ in His believers is added together, the sum equals the church. Therefore, we all must put off our old man. We need to put off all the natural life until the living Christ can be expressed from within our spirit. Then we will be the church in reality. In the church, the new man, there is no Jew, Greek, or barbarian, but Christ is all and in all (Col. 3:11). To live out anything other than Christ is not the church. "It is no longer I who live, but it is Christ who lives in me" (Gal. 2:20). "For to me, to live is Christ" (Phil. 1:21). This is the church!

Consider the picture depicted in the four Gospels. When the Lord Jesus came as the last Adam and looked at the Jewish religionists, He seemed to say of them, "This is a horse and that is a turtle." In Matthew 16 He turned to Peter and said, "Satan." The Lord seemed to be saying, "These are not My counterpart. They do not match Me. They can never be My complement." Thus, the Lord Jesus had to die. He had to sleep on the cross that He might release His life to produce His real complement to match Him. After He awoke from death in resurrection, He saw the church. At that time, especially on the day of Pentecost, He could say, "This time this is bone of My bones and flesh of My flesh."

Only that which comes out of Christ can be recognized by Christ. Only that which comes out of Christ can return to Christ and match Him. Only that which comes out of the resurrection life of Christ can be His complement and counterpart, the Body of Christ. Only that which comes out of Christ and which is Christ Himself can be one with Christ. (*Life-study of Genesis*, pp. 221-222)

Further Reading: Life-study of Genesis, msg. 17

Enlightenment and inspiration: _____

_____

_____

_____

Morning Nourishment

Eph. For no one ever hated his own flesh, but nourishes and
5:29-30 cherishes it, even as Christ also the church, because
we are members of His Body.
   32 This mystery is great, but I speak with regard to Christ
and the church.
Rev. And I saw the holy city, New Jerusalem, coming down
21:2 out of heaven from God, prepared as a bride adorned
for her husband.

The Epistles reveal that after the day of Pentecost many negative things crept in. The "animals," such as the horse and the turtle, appeared once again. Thus, the Lord Jesus had to say again, "This is not and that is not." Now He is waiting for the coming wedding. At that wedding day He will look at the overcomers and say, "This time it is bone of My bones and flesh of My flesh."

As we are on our way toward that wedding feast we must cast off all the natural things, the things of the natural man, the things other than Christ....Many times...the life within says, "This is not," but even more times the resurrection life says, "This is it." We need to hear the voice of Christ, the resurrection life within us, and to go along with it all the time. (*Life-study of Genesis,* pp. 222-223)

Today's Reading

In typology, Adam and Eve became one flesh (Gen. 2:23-24). In actuality, Christ and the church are one spirit, because he that is joined to the Lord is one spirit (1 Cor. 6:17). Figuratively speaking, all the believers of Christ are "members of His Body." The marriage union between husband and wife is a great mystery "with regard to Christ and the church" (Eph. 5:29-32).

In Genesis 2 we see the creation of man and the tree of life, which denotes God as man's life and life supply. As God works Himself into man, man begins to experience the flow of life, and at the flow of life there are the precious materials—gold, pearl, and onyx stone. At the end of Genesis 2 we see the building of a woman. All the precious materials mentioned earlier in this chapter are for the building of this woman. If we only have Genesis 2, we cannot understand this matter adequately and clearly. However, at the end of the Bible we also find a woman, the New Jerusalem. This woman is a city built with gold, pearl, and precious stones. In Genesis 2, these materials were found at the flow of life, but were not yet builded. At the end of the Bible all of these materials have been built up into a city, which is the ultimate and eternal woman. In Genesis 2 we can see the New Jerusalem foreshadowed by Eve and in Revelation 21 we can see Eve consummated in the New Jerusalem, the corporate bride of the Lamb built with the three precious materials.

The result of Christ's death with His side pierced to release His divine life was that He obtained the church as His complement. Henceforth, God is no longer alone. Christ has gained a bride to match Him. Revelation 21—22 unfolds that in eternity the New Jerusalem as the consummation of the church will be the bride of Christ for God's full complement to match Him eternally.

Adam and Eve eventually became one flesh, one complete unit. This was a figure of God and man being joined as one. God's desire is to be one with man. He has reached this goal through Christ's death and resurrection which produced the church, representing the proper humanity to match Him as the husband. In this union humanity is one with divinity; this union will last for eternity. The coming New Jerusalem will be just the unity of God and man, a living, complete unit composed with divinity and humanity.

Adam and Eve, being one, lived together. This portrayed that God, the universal husband, will live with regenerated humanity forever. The universal marriage life of God and man is fully revealed in Revelation 21. In eternity, God in Christ will be the center, reality, and life of man's living, and man will live by God in Christ as life. Man will express God's glory and will exercise God's authority over the new earth. God and man, man and God will live together in a marriage life forever. (*Life-study of Genesis*, pp. 223-225)

Further Reading: Life-study of Genesis, msg. 17

Enlightenment and inspiration: _____

_____

_____

_____

Hymns, #1058

1 Rock of Ages, cleft for me,
Let me hide myself in Thee;
Let the water and the blood,
From Thy riven side which flowed,
Be of sin the double cure,
Save me from its guilt and power.

2 Not the labor of my hands
Can fulfill Thy law's demands;
Could my zeal no respite know,
Could my tears forever flow,
All could never sin erase,
Thou must save, and save by grace.

3 Nothing in my hands I bring,
Simply to Thy cross I cling;
Naked, come to Thee for dress,
Helpless, look to Thee for grace:
Foul, I to the fountain fly,
Wash me, Savior, or I die.

4 While I draw this fleeting breath,
When mine eyes shall close in death,
When I soar to worlds unknown,
See Thee on Thy judgment throne,
Rock of Ages, cleft for me,
Let me hide myself in Thee.

Composition for prophecy with main point and sub-points: _____

_____
_____
_____
_____
_____
_____
_____
_____
_____
_____
_____
_____
_____
_____
_____
_____
_____
_____
_____
_____
_____
_____
_____
_____
_____
_____
_____
_____
_____
_____
_____
_____
_____
_____
_____
_____
_____
_____
_____

The Fourth Great Pillar—the Gospel
(2)
The Center of Paul's Gospel

Scripture Reading: Rom. 1:1, 3-4, 9, 15-16; 2:16; 8:2-3, 9-11, 28-30; 16:25

Day 1   **I. The book of Galatians presents the basic truth of the gospel (2:5, 14):**

A. The first aspect of the truth of the gospel is that fallen man cannot be justified out of works of law (v. 16a).

B. Under God's New Testament economy, we are justified out of faith in Christ (v. 16b):

1. Through believing, we are joined to Christ and become one with Him (John 3:15).

2. Faith in Christ denotes an organic union with Him through believing; the term *in Christ* refers to this organic union (Gal. 2:17; 3:14, 28; 5:6).

3. Justification is not merely a matter of position; it is also an organic matter, a matter in life.

4. It is by means of our organic union with Christ that God can reckon Christ as our righteousness; only in this way can we be justified by God (1 Cor. 1:30).

Day 2   **II. Paul's gospel is the unique gospel, the complete gospel (Rom. 16:25):**

A. Paul's gospel includes all the aspects of the gospel in the four Gospels:

1. In Matthew the goal of the gospel of the kingdom is to bring people into God to make them citizens of the kingdom of the heavens (28:19; 24:14; Rom. 14:17; Gal. 5:21).

2. In Mark the preaching of the gospel is to bring part of the old creation into the new creation (16:15-16; Rom. 8:20-21; Gal. 6:15).

3. In Luke we have the gospel of forgiveness to bring redeemed people back to the God-ordained

blessing (24:46-47; 1:77-79; 2:30-32; Eph. 1:3, 7; Gal. 3:14).

    4. In John we have the eternal life so that we may bear fruit for the building up of the Body of Christ, which is Christ's increase (20:31; 15:16; Rom. 8:10, 6, 11; 12:4-5; Gal. 3:28; 4:19; 6:10, 16).

  B. Paul's gospel is the center of the New Testament revelation (Rom. 1:1, 9):

    1. Paul's gospel is a revelation of the Triune God, processed to become the all-inclusive life-giving Spirit (1 Cor. 15:45b; 2 Cor. 3:17; Gal. 3:2, 5, 14).

Day 3

    2. Paul's gospel is centered on the Triune God being our life in order to be one with us and to make us one with Him, that we may be the Body of Christ to express Christ in a corporate way (Rom. 8:11; 12:4-5; Eph. 1:22-23).

III. **Paul's gospel includes the entire book of Romans (2:16; 16:25):**

  A. The gospel of God, as the subject of the book of Romans, concerns Christ as the Spirit living within the believers after His resurrection (8:10-11):

    1. This is higher and more subjective than what was presented in the Gospels, which mainly concern Christ in the flesh as He lived among His disciples after His incarnation but before His death and resurrection (John 1:14; 14:17).

    2. The Epistle to the Romans reveals that Christ has resurrected and has become the life-giving Spirit, and as such, He is no longer merely the Christ outside the believers, but He is now the Christ within them (8:9-11).

    3. The gospel in the book of Romans is the gospel of the One who is now indwelling His believers as their subjective Savior (1:3-4, 15-16; 8:10).

  B. The entire book of Romans, from chapter 1 on the person of Jesus Christ the God-man and on the righteousness of God to chapter 16 on the local churches as the expression of the Body of Christ, is the gospel of God in its completeness (1:1, 3-4, 9, 16-17; 12:4-5; 16:1, 4, 16).

C. As revealed in Romans, Paul's gospel is a gospel of sonship (8:14, 29; Gal. 3:26; 4:7):

1. The central concept of the gospel of God is related to the Son of God, and God's intention is to bring many sons into glory (Rom. 1:3-4; 8:3, 29; Heb. 2:10).

2. God predestinated us unto sonship; the choosing of God's people to be holy is for the purpose of their being made sons of God, participating in the divine sonship (Eph. 1:4-5; Rom. 8:28-30).

D. We need to preach the gospel in Romans in a way that will cause people to realize the following:

1. That once they believe in the Lord, their sins will be forgiven, and they will be redeemed and justified by God, reconciled to God, and accepted by God (3:20, 23-28; 5:1-2, 8, 10, 17).

2. That they will be regenerated in the spirit, have God's life and nature, and have God dwelling in them to renew and transform them so that they may be conformed to the image of God's Son and eventually reach the maturity in life and be fully glorified as sons of God (8:2, 9-11, 16, 29-30).

3. That although they are sinners, they will become sons of God and members of Christ, coordinating together to constitute the Body of Christ, which is the testimony and the expression of Christ expressed practically on earth as the local churches (12:1-2, 4-5, 11; 16:1, 4, 16).

IV. **The center of Paul's gospel is Romans 8, which concerns the dispensing of the Triune God as life into the tripartite man (vv. 2, 6, 10-11):**

A. The Bible reveals the mystery of God, the mystery of the universe, the mystery of man, the mystery of the church, and the mystery of the future; within the Bible, Romans 8 is the mystery of all mysteries, for it particularly unveils and explains these five mysteries (vv. 1-2, 4, 6, 9-11, 17-25, 28-30).

B. Romans 8 reveals the focal point of God's economy—that in eternity past God purposed to enter into His chosen and redeemed people so that He could be their life and they could be His corporate expression (vv. 10-11, 28-30).

C. Romans 8, an experiential chapter, speaks about the Triune God in the experience of the Christian life (vv. 2, 10-11).

Day 6

D. The law of the Spirit of life is uniquely revealed in Romans 8; the law of the Spirit of life is the Triune God in motion; when the Triune God moves within us, He is the law of the Spirit of life (vv. 2, 10-11).

E. Romans 8 concerns the wonderful, all-inclusive life-giving Spirit as the ultimate consummation of the Triune God; this Spirit will make us exactly the same as Christ is in life, nature, and expression (vv. 2, 9, 11, 13-14, 16, 23).

F. The purpose of the all-inclusive Spirit being life to our spirit, mind, and body is that we would be conformed to the image of God's firstborn Son; this conformation is the goal of the working of the divine life within us (vv. 2, 6, 10-11, 29).

G. Romans 8 is central because it concerns God's goal and our destiny—conformation to the image of the firstborn Son of God; eventually, we will be fully conformed to the image of God's firstborn Son for the eternal, corporate expression of the Triune God (v. 29; 12:4-5; Rev. 21:10-11).

Morning Nourishment

Gal. To them we yielded with the subjection *demanded*
2:5 not even for an hour, that the truth of the gospel
      might remain with you.
16 And knowing that a man is not justified out of works
      of law, but through faith in Jesus Christ...
1 Cor. But of Him you are in Christ Jesus, who became
1:30 wisdom to us from God: both righteousness and sanc-
      tification and redemption.

In Galatians 2:5 and 14 Paul speaks of the truth of the gospel.
The word *truth* in these verses does not mean the doctrine or
teaching of the gospel; it denotes the reality of the gospel.
Although Galatians is a short book, it affords us a complete revelation of the reality of the gospel. This revelation, however, is
given not in detail but in certain basic principles. Therefore, in
this message we shall cover the truth of the gospel revealed in
these basic principles.

The first aspect of the truth of the gospel is that fallen man cannot be justified by works of law. In 2:16 Paul says, "Knowing that a
man is not justified out of works of law." At the end of this verse Paul
declares, "Out of the works of law no flesh will be justified." The
word *flesh* in 2:16 means fallen man who has become flesh (Gen.
6:3). No such man will be justified by works of law. Furthermore, in
Galatians 3:11 Paul goes on to say, "And that by law no one is justified before God is evident." In these verses Paul tells us clearly that
no one is justified by works of law. (*Life-study of Galatians,* p. 69)

Today's Reading

Under God's New Testament economy, we are not to keep the
law. On the contrary, we are justified by faith in Christ (Gal. 2:16).
...What actually is faith in Christ, and what does it mean to be
justified by faith in Christ? Faith in Christ denotes an organic
union through believing.

This faith creates an organic union in which we and Christ are
one. Therefore, the expression "by faith in Christ" actually denotes
an organic union accomplished by believing in Christ. The term

"in Christ" refers to this organic union. Before we believed in Christ, there was a great separation between us and Christ. We were we, and Christ was Christ. But through believing we were joined to Christ and became one with Him. Now we are in Christ, and Christ is in us. This is an organic union, a union in life. This union is illustrated by the grafting of a branch of one tree into another tree. Through faith in Christ we are grafted into Christ. Through this process of spiritual grafting, two lives are grafted and become one.

Many Christians have a shallow understanding of justification by faith. How could Christ be our righteousness if we were not organically united to Him? It is by means of our organic union with Christ that God can reckon Christ as our righteousness. Because we and Christ are one, whatever belongs to Him is ours. This is the basis upon which God counts Christ as our righteousness.

Marriage is a helpful illustration of this, although it is inadequate. Suppose a poor woman is united in marriage to a wealthy man. Through this union she participates in the wealth of her husband. In like manner, through our organic union with Christ, we share whatever Christ is and has. As soon as this union takes place, in the eyes of God Christ becomes us, and we become one with Him. Only in this way can we be justified before God.

Many Christians have a mere doctrinal understanding of justification by faith. According to their concept, Christ is the just One, the righteous One on the throne in the presence of God. When we believe in Christ, God reckons Christ to be our righteousness. This understanding of justification is very shallow....In order to be justified by faith in Christ, we need to believe in the Lord Jesus out of an appreciation of His preciousness. As Christ's preciousness is infused into us through the preaching of the gospel, we spontaneously appreciate the Lord and call on Him....Through such a believing we and Christ become one. Therefore, God must reckon Him as our righteousness. (*Life-study of Galatians,* pp. 72, 74-75)

Further Reading: Life-study of Galatians, msgs. 8-9

__Enlightenment and inspiration:__ _____

_____

_____

_____

Morning Nourishment

Rom. Now to Him who is able to establish you according to
16:25 my gospel, that is, the proclamation of Jesus Christ,
       according to the revelation of the mystery, which has
       been kept in silence in the times of the ages.
Gal. He therefore who bountifully supplies to you the Spirit
3:5   and does works of power among you, *does He do it* out
      of the works of law or out of the hearing of faith?

The gospel preached by the apostle Paul was the unique gospel. It was the gospel of Christ (Gal. 1:7).

Paul's gospel includes all the aspects of the first four Gospels. In his writings Paul speaks of the kingdom, life, forgiveness, and service. However, in his Epistles he covers much more. In Colossians 1:25 Paul says that he became a minister according to the stewardship of God to complete the word of God. Hence, Paul's gospel is the gospel of completion. Without Paul's gospel, the revelation of the gospel in the New Testament would not be complete. (*Life-study of Galatians,* pp. 18, 14)

Today's Reading

All the authority in heaven and on earth...has been given to God's Christ. This authority given to Christ is for the establishing of the kingdom of the heavens. In Matthew the Lord is the King-Savior who commissioned His disciples to go and disciple the nations by baptizing them into the name of the Father and of the Son and of the Holy Spirit. This is to bring the people out from the nations into the Triune God. The intrinsic purpose of our preaching the gospel is to bring people of the nations into the Triune God, to make them the citizens of the kingdom of the heavens.

In His resurrection the Lord as the Slave-Savior charged His disciples to go into all the world and proclaim the gospel to all the creation (of which mankind is the main item) to redeem and save God's lost creation from the vanity and slavery of corruption back to Him to enjoy the freedom of His glory (Mark 16:14-15; Rom. 8:20-21) in His new creation (Gal. 6:15b)....Mankind takes the lead of all the creation. Mark reveals that we preach the gospel to make people of the old creation the members of the new creation.

In Matthew the Lord is the King-Savior. In Mark He is the Slave-Savior to serve people that they may be redeemed and saved back to God. In Luke He is the Man-Savior. After the accomplishment of God's redemption for man through His death and resurrection, the Lord as the Man-Savior charged His disciples to proclaim repentance for forgiveness of sins in His name to all the nations that the fallen men may be redeemed back to the way of peace that leads them into the blessing prepared by God for them according to His eternal economy (Luke 24:46-48; 1:77-79; 2:30-32). In Mark it is the fallen creation, but in Luke it is the fallen men who need to be redeemed back to the way of peace.

In the four Gospels, the Lord is revealed as the King-Savior, the Slave-Savior, the Man-Savior, and the God-Savior respectively. In the Gospel of John, we see the mingling of the Triune God with the believers to produce the Body of Christ. We are the members of Christ just as we are the branches of the vine tree to bear fruit for the building up of the Body of Christ, which is Christ's increase. The Body of Christ will consummate in the New Jerusalem for God's eternal enlargement and expression. (*Crystallization-study of the Epistle to the Romans,* pp. 285-287)

Paul's Epistles not only complete the divine revelation; they form the very heart of God's revelation in the New Testament. Thus, Paul's gospel is not only the gospel of completion; it is also the center of the New Testament revelation. For this reason, Paul's gospel is the basic gospel.

Many Christians today are not clear about this matter either. They may be familiar with the councils, the creeds, and the teachings of the historic church, but they do not know Paul's revelation of the Triune God processed to become the all-inclusive Spirit. This indicates that few Christians adequately know the gospel according to Paul. (*Life-study of Galatians,* pp. 16-17)

Further Reading: Life-study of Galatians, msg. 2; *Crystallization-study of the Epistle to the Romans,* msg. 26

Enlightenment and inspiration: _____

_____

_____

_____

Morning Nourishment

Rom.   For I am not ashamed of the gospel, for it is the power
1:16-17 of God unto salvation to everyone who believes, both
to Jew first and to Greek. For the righteousness of God
is revealed in it out of faith to faith, as it is written,
"But the righteous shall have life and live by faith."

The apostle received the gospel through the revelation of
Christ. Here the revelation of Christ does not refer merely to a
revelation received through Jesus Christ or to the revelation concerning Christ. Rather, it refers to the person of Christ, who was
revealed in the apostle. Paul received the gospel through such a
personal revelation. Revelation is the opening of the veil in order
to show something hidden from view. One day God opened the
veil to Paul, and he immediately saw the revealed Christ. (*The
Conclusion of the New Testament,* p. 3258)

Today's Reading

The gospel that the apostle received through the revelation of
Christ is the center of God's revelation in the New Testament (Rom.
1:1, 9). Paul's gospel is a revelation of the Triune God processed to
become the all-inclusive life-giving Spirit (1 Cor. 15:45b; 2 Cor. 3:17;
Gal. 3:2, 5, 14). His gospel is centered on the Triune God being our
life in order to be one with us and to make us one with Him so that
we may be the Body of Christ to express Christ in a corporate way
(Rom. 8:11; 12:4-5; Eph. 1:22-23). The focal point of Paul's gospel is
God Himself in His Trinity becoming the processed all-inclusive Spirit
to be life and everything to us for our enjoyment so that He and we
may be one to express Him for eternity (Gal. 4:4, 6; 3:13-14, 26-28;
6:15). (*The Conclusion of the New Testament,* p. 3258)

The gospel of God is the entire book of Romans, comprising sixteen chapters. When I was young, I considered that only the first
three chapters of Romans were concerning the gospel. From verse 18
of chapter one through verse 20 of chapter three we see God's condemnation on ungodly and unrighteous mankind. Because all of
us are sinners, we need the Lord Jesus' redemption. Therefore,
the end of chapter three reveals that we are justified by faith and

redeemed in Christ. In the past I considered that chapters four through sixteen of Romans were not the preaching of the gospel but were words of edification....[But], Paul indicates that the entire book of Romans is the gospel of God. (*The Advance of the Lord's Recovery Today,* p. 20)

The complete salvation of God in the book of Romans is carried out on and brought into the believers of Christ by the power of God through His complete gospel (Rom. 1:16, 1). *Power of God* in Romans 1:16 denotes a powerful force that can break through any obstacle. This power is the resurrected Christ Himself, who is the life-giving Spirit, and it is unto salvation to everyone who believes.

The gospel of God, as the subject of Romans, concerns Christ as the Spirit living within the believers after His resurrection. This is higher and more subjective than what was presented in the Gospels, which concern Christ only in the flesh as He lived among His disciples after His incarnation but before His death and resurrection. This book, however, reveals that Christ has resurrected and has become the life-giving Spirit (8:9-10). He is no longer merely the Christ outside the believers, but He is now the Christ within them. Hence, the gospel in this book is the gospel of the One who is now indwelling His believers as their subjective Savior. (*Crystallization-study of the Complete Salvation of God in Romans,* p. 9)

Romans is a book on the gospel of God (1:1). The entire book, from chapter one on the person of Jesus Christ the God-man and on the righteousness of God to chapter sixteen on the local churches as the expression of the Body of Christ, is the gospel, the good news and the glad tidings (Rom. 10:15), of God to men in its completeness. No other book presents us the gospel of God in such a complete way as Romans does. Do not think that only the first four chapters of Romans on justification by faith are the gospel of God....You have to realize that every chapter in this book is a part of the gospel of God. (*Crystallization-study of the Epistle to the Romans,* p. 4)

Further Reading: Crystallization-study of the Epistle to the Romans, msg. 1; *The Conclusion of the New Testament,* msg. 324

Enlightenment and inspiration: _____

_____

_____

_____

Morning Nourishment

Rom.   ...The gospel of God...concerning His Son, who came
1:1, 3-4 out of the seed of David according to the flesh, who
was designated the Son of God in power according to
the Spirit of holiness out of the resurrection of the
dead, Jesus Christ our Lord.

Heb.   For it was fitting for Him, for whom are all things and
2:10   through whom are all things, in leading many sons
into glory...

We have seen that we are to serve God in the gospel of His Son
(Rom. 1:9). This gospel is a gospel of sonship. Sonship includes
designation, resurrection, justification, sanctification, transformation, conformation, glorification, and manifestation. We are
presently undergoing the process of designation; that is, we are
being designated sons of God by the power of resurrection. Sonship is for the Body. In order to be members of the Body of Christ,
we must be sons of God. (*Life-study of Romans*, p. 617)

Today's Reading

In our reading of Romans we may pay attention to condemnation, justification, sanctification, and glorification, but neglect the
matters of sonship, transformation, conformation, and the Body
life. The central thought of Romans is not condemnation nor justification; it is not even sanctification nor glorification. In 1:1 and 3
Paul says that he was separated unto the gospel of God concerning God's Son. This indicates that the central concept of the gospel
of God is related to the Son of God. God's intention is to bring
many sons into glory.

According to the Bible, the spiritual significance of sonship is
that a son is the expression of his father. God desires to have many
sons because His intention is to have Himself expressed in a corporate way. He does not want simply an individual expression in
the only begotten Son, but a Body expression, a corporate expression, in many sons. John 1:18 says, "No one has ever seen God; the
only begotten Son, who is in the bosom of the Father, He has
declared Him." Although God's expression in the only begotten

Son is marvelous, God still desires an expression in many sons. His intention is to make the only begotten Son the Firstborn among many brothers. Before the resurrection of Christ, God had just one Son; that is, He had an individual expression. But by means of Christ's resurrection, God now has a multitude of sons; that is, He has a corporate expression. (*Life-study of Romans,* p. 549)

The choosing of God's people for them to be holy is for the purpose of their being made sons of God, participating in the divine sonship [Eph. 1:5; Rom. 8:23, 29; Gal. 4:5-6]. (*The Issue of the Dispensing of the Processed Trinity and the Transmitting of the Transcending Christ,* p. 13)

If what we preach is merely about escaping perdition and going to "heaven," then we are preaching the poorest gospel. We must preach the gospel in a way that allows people to clearly see that once they believe in the Lord, their sins will be forgiven, and they will be redeemed and justified by God, reconciled to God, and accepted by God. They should also see that at the same time they will be regenerated in their spirit, have God's life and nature, and have God dwelling in their spirit to renew them day by day and transform them moment by moment. This is so that they may be conformed to the image of His Son and eventually reach the maturity in life and be fully glorified as the sons of God....They are members of Christ, coordinating together to constitute the Body of Christ, which is the testimony, the riches, and the expression of Christ expressed practically on the earth as the local churches. This is the gospel in Romans.

[The book of Romans] is concerning the complete gospel of God, beginning with forgiveness of sins, passing through sanctification, transformation, and the constitution of the Body of Christ, and eventually arriving at the living of the church life in the churches. (*Truth, Life, the Church, and the Gospel—the Four Great Pillars in the Lord's Recovery,* p. 122)

Further Reading: Life-study of Romans, msgs. 52-53; *Truth, Life, the Church, and the Gospel—the Four Great Pillars in the Lord's Recovery,* ch. 10

Enlightenment and inspiration: _____

_____

_____

_____

Morning Nourishment

Rom. But if Christ is in you, though the body is dead
8:10-11 because of sin, the spirit is life because of righteousness. And if the Spirit of the One who raised Jesus
from the dead dwells in you, He who raised Christ
from the dead will also give life to your mortal bodies
through His Spirit who indwells you.

Romans 8 is the center of Paul's gospel, which is concerning
the Triune God dispensing Himself into the tripartite man. Hence,
in this chapter Paul mentions the Father, the Son, and the Spirit
(vv. 9-11). God is the Triune God—the Father, the Son, and the
Spirit—for the purpose of dispensing Himself into man. We
human beings are tripartite, having a spirit, soul, and body.…
Romans 8 tells us that the Triune God first enters into our spirit
(v. 10), then saturates our mind from our spirit, that is, enters into
our soul (v. 6), and then enters into our body, giving life to our mortal bodies (v. 11). In this way, our tripartite being—our spirit, soul,
and body—is filled with God.…This is the gospel of God. (*Truth,
Life, the Church, and the Gospel—the Four Great Pillars in the
Lord's Recovery*, pp. 122-123)

Today's Reading

To preach the gospel is to tell people that God wants to enter
into man and make sinners sons of God, that these sons of God
are living members of Christ for the constitution of the church,
and that these ones are in the church, which is expressed in different localities, so that they can live the church life in the local
churches. (*Truth, Life, the Church, and the Gospel—the Four Great
Pillars in the Lord's Recovery*, p. 123)

The Bible is a book of mystery, containing at least five main
mysteries—God, the universe, man, the church, and the future.
Any thoughtful person would be puzzled by these five mysteries.
Many have wondered, "Does God exist? Who is God? What are
God's attributes?" The universe is a mystery, for its dimensions
are immeasurable. Man is a mystery in more than one sense. Corporately, human beings throughout the earth are busy doing

various things, but very few know the real meaning, the purpose, of human existence. Individually, each person is a mystery. Even husbands and wives do not understand one another, nor do parents understand their children. The church is a mystery as well, especially in its definition and purpose. Finally, the future of the universe, mankind, the church, and even God is a mystery. The answer to all these mysteries is in the Bible. The Bible reveals the mystery of God, the mystery of the universe, the mystery of man, the mystery of the church, and the mystery of the future. Within the Bible, Romans 8 is the mystery of all the mysteries, for it particularly unveils and explains these five mysteries.

Romans 8 reveals that the Spirit of life, the law of the Spirit of life, the Spirit of God, the Spirit of Christ, and the Spirit of the resurrecting One are all one in the Spirit, who is life to our spirit, mind, and body. Nothing is more precious than these aspects of the all-inclusive Spirit, which meet our every need and completely satisfy us. (*The All-inclusive Indwelling Spirit,* pp. 7, 17)

In eternity past God purposed a plan. According to this plan, He created the universe with the heavens, the earth, and billions of items....[Then] man was created not to be an instrument but a vessel to contain God so that God may be expressed from within man. This is God's eternal plan, His eternal purpose. (*Life-study of Ephesians,* pp. 81-82)

Romans 8:3 says that God, referring to the Father, sent His Son. Furthermore, Romans 8 mentions the Spirit in at least ten verses (vv. 2, 5, 9, 11, 13, 14, 16, 23, 26, 27). Thus, this chapter reveals the Triune God. However, Romans 8 is not a doctrinal chapter but an experiential chapter. It speaks not about the doctrine of the Trinity but about the Trinity in the experience of the Christian life. God is triune to be experienced by us. We are able to experience God because He is triune as the Father, the Son, and the Spirit. (*The All-inclusive Indwelling Spirit,* pp. 7-8)

Further Reading: The All-inclusive Indwelling Spirit, chs. 1-2; Life-study of Ephesians, msg. 9

Enlightenment and inspiration: _____

Morning Nourishment

Rom. For the law of the Spirit of life has freed me in Christ
8:2 Jesus from the law of sin and of death.
29 Because those whom He foreknew, He also predestinated *to be* conformed to the image of His Son, that
He might be the Firstborn among many brothers.

Romans 8:2 mentions the law of the Spirit of life, which is not
the Mosaic law or any written law but a natural law, a natural
power that works automatically....Almost two thousand years
ago, before the development of science, the apostle Paul received a
revelation from God of the law of the Spirit of life and was able to
describe it in scientific terms. Within us is the powerful law of the
Spirit of life. (*The All-inclusive Indwelling Spirit*, pp. 8-9)

Today's Reading

Resurrection and life are a person, and now this person is the
Spirit. Moreover, today this person is also a law—the law of
the Spirit of life. The law of the Spirit of life, which is uniquely
revealed in Romans 8, is nothing less than the Triune God in
motion. When the Triune God moves within us, He is the law of
the Spirit of life. The Triune God works in us not by accident or
activity but as a law. Once electricity is installed in a building, it
works as a law, not by activity or accident. When the people in a
building need light, they do not need to petition the power plant.
Instead, they need only to switch on the light. Some Christians
believe that in order to receive the Spirit, they must fast and pray
for a long time....However, today the Spirit functions according
to a law....As long as we have believed in the Lord and called on
His name, the Triune God as the heavenly "electricity" has been
installed in us and works automatically and powerfully as the law
of the Spirit of life.

The goal of the Spirit's working within us is to renew, transform, and conform us in every avenue and corner of our being.

Romans 8 concerns the wonderful, all-inclusive life-giving Spirit
as the ultimate consummation of the processed Triune God. This
Spirit is now infusing life into our entire being from our spirit into

our mind, the leading part of our soul, and eventually into our entire body—resurrecting, renewing, transforming, and conforming us to the glorious image of the firstborn Son of God, Jesus Christ, who is both the Son of God and the Son of Man. The Spirit will make us exactly the same as Christ is in life, nature, and expression. This is Romans 8.

The purpose of the all-inclusive Spirit being life to our spirit, mind, and body is revealed in verse 29, which says, "Those whom He [God] foreknew, He also predestinated to be conformed to the image of His Son, that He might be the Firstborn among many brothers." Before the foundation of the world, God knew each one of us and loved us in spite of our flaws, defects, and sinfulness. God loves us without reason. Real love has no reason. If love has a reason, it is political. God foreknew us, and because He loved us, He predestinated us to be conformed to the image of His firstborn Son. To predestinate is to mark out beforehand. Our destiny is to be conformed to the image of God's firstborn Son. This conformation is the goal of the working of the divine life within us. God made our spirit life at regeneration and is now making our mind life and even working life into our body for His purpose—to conform us fallen sinners to the image of Christ, the firstborn Son of God.

Romans 8 is central because it concerns God's goal and our destiny—our conformation to Christ's image. God is accomplishing this goal, and we will reach this destiny. One day we will no longer be flawed and sinful. Today we are in the process, which means that we still have many defects and shortcomings, but we can be assured that we will eventually be fully conformed to the image, the expression, of God's firstborn Son. We will be the same as Christ is. When we are fully conformed, we will express Christ perfectly. Our sinful nature and all our defects will be swallowed up as we are transformed into the same image from glory to glory (2 Cor. 3:18). (*The All-inclusive Indwelling Spirit*, pp. 9-10, 20, 17-18)

Further Reading: A Deeper Study of the Divine Dispensing, chs. 3-6; Conformation to the Image of the Son of God, chs. 1-2

Enlightenment and inspiration: _____

_____

_____

Hymns, #1213

1   If from your nat'ral man you would be free,
      Amen the law of life!
  This law works in us automatically,
      Amen the law of life!
      Amen the law of life!
      Amen the law of life!
  This law transforms us, to Christ conforms us—
      Amen the law of life!

2   From life divine it does originate,
      Amen the law of life!
  Its function, working, power are innate,
      Amen the law of life!
      Amen the law of life!
      Amen the law of life!
  Stop all your trying, on life relying,
      Amen the law of life!

3   The law of life fulfills our God's desire,
      Amen the law of life!
  Our self-improvement He does not require,
      Amen the law of life!
      Amen the law of life!
      Amen the law of life!
  God's plan fulfilling; Yes, Lord, we're willing,
      Amen the law of life!

4   This law transforms us metabolically,
      Amen the law of life!
  'Til we are permeated corporately,
      Amen the law of life!
      Amen the law of life!
      Amen the law of life!
  Old man denying, God's life supplying,
      Amen the law of life!

5   This law's inscribing Christ upon our hearts,
      Amen the law of life!
  'Til He is written in our inward parts,
      Amen the law of life!
      Amen the law of life!
      Amen the law of life!
  Christ's form engraving, not mere behaving,
      Amen the law of life!

Composition for prophecy with main point and sub-points: _____

Reading Schedule for the Recovery Version of the Old Testament with Footnotes

Wk.	Lord's Day	Monday	Tuesday	Wednesday	Thursday	Friday	Saturday
1	☐ Gen 1:1-5	☐ 1:6-23	☐ 1:24-31	☐ 2:1-9	☐ 2:10-25	☐ 3:1-13	☐ 3:14-24
2	☐ 4:1-26	☐ 5:1-32	☐ 6:1-22	☐ 7:1—8:3	☐ 8:4-22	☐ 9:1-29	☐ 10:1-32
3	☐ 11:1-32	☐ 12:1-20	☐ 13:1-18	☐ 14:1-24	☐ 15:1-21	☐ 16:1-16	☐ 17:1-27
4	☐ 18:1-33	☐ 19:1-38	☐ 20:1-18	☐ 21:1-34	☐ 22:1-24	☐ 23:1—24:27	☐ 24:28-67
5	☐ 25:1-34	☐ 26:1-35	☐ 27:1-46	☐ 28:1-22	☐ 29:1-35	☐ 30:1-43	☐ 31:1-55
6	☐ 32:1-32	☐ 33:1—34:31	☐ 35:1-29	☐ 36:1-43	☐ 37:1-36	☐ 38:1—39:23	☐ 40:1—41:13
7	☐ 41:14-57	☐ 42:1-38	☐ 43:1-34	☐ 44:1-34	☐ 45:1-28	☐ 46:1-34	☐ 47:1-31
8	☐ 48:1-22	☐ 49:1-15	☐ 49:16-33	☐ 50:1-26	☐ Exo 1:1-22	☐ 2:1-25	☐ 3:1-22
9	☐ 4:1-31	☐ 5:1-23	☐ 6:1-30	☐ 7:1-25	☐ 8:1-32	☐ 9:1-35	☐ 10:1-29
10	☐ 11:1-10	☐ 12:1-14	☐ 12:15-36	☐ 12:37-51	☐ 13:1-22	☐ 14:1-31	☐ 15:1-27
11	☐ 16:1-36	☐ 17:1-16	☐ 18:1-27	☐ 19:1-25	☐ 20:1-26	☐ 21:1-36	☐ 22:1-31
12	☐ 23:1-33	☐ 24:1-18	☐ 25:1-22	☐ 25:23-40	☐ 26:1-14	☐ 26:15-37	☐ 27:1-21
13	☐ 28:1-21	☐ 28:22-43	☐ 29:1-21	☐ 29:22-46	☐ 30:1-10	☐ 30:11-38	☐ 31:1-17
14	☐ 31:18—32:35	☐ 33:1-23	☐ 34:1-35	☐ 35:1-35	☐ 36:1-38	☐ 37:1-29	☐ 38:1-31
15	☐ 39:1-43	☐ 40:1-38	☐ Lev 1:1-17	☐ 2:1-16	☐ 3:1-17	☐ 4:1-35	☐ 5:1-19
16	☐ 6:1-30	☐ 7:1-38	☐ 8:1-36	☐ 9:1-24	☐ 10:1-20	☐ 11:1-47	☐ 12:1-8
17	☐ 13:1-28	☐ 13:29-59	☐ 14:1-18	☐ 14:19-32	☐ 14:33-57	☐ 15:1-33	☐ 16:1-17
18	☐ 16:18-34	☐ 17:1-16	☐ 18:1-30	☐ 19:1-37	☐ 20:1-27	☐ 21:1-24	☐ 22:1-33
19	☐ 23:1-22	☐ 23:23-44	☐ 24:1-23	☐ 25:1-23	☐ 25:24-55	☐ 26:1-24	☐ 26:25-46
20	☐ 27:1-34	☐ Num 1:1-54	☐ 2:1-34	☐ 3:1-51	☐ 4:1-49	☐ 5:1-31	☐ 6:1-27
21	☐ 7:1-41	☐ 7:42-88	☐ 7:89—8:26	☐ 9:1-23	☐ 10:1-36	☐ 11:1-35	☐ 12:1—13:33
22	☐ 14:1-45	☐ 15:1-41	☐ 16:1-50	☐ 17:1—18:7	☐ 18:8-32	☐ 19:1-22	☐ 20:1-29
23	☐ 21:1-35	☐ 22:1-41	☐ 23:1-30	☐ 24:1-25	☐ 25:1-18	☐ 26:1-65	☐ 27:1-23
24	☐ 28:1-31	☐ 29:1-40	☐ 30:1—31:24	☐ 31:25-54	☐ 32:1-42	☐ 33:1-56	☐ 34:1-29
25	☐ 35:1-34	☐ 36:1-13	☐ Deut 1:1-46	☐ 2:1-37	☐ 3:1-29	☐ 4:1-49	☐ 5:1-33
26	☐ 6:1—7:26	☐ 8:1-20	☐ 9:1-29	☐ 10:1-22	☐ 11:1-32	☐ 12:1-32	☐ 13:1—14:21

Reading Schedule for the Recovery Version of the Old Testament with Footnotes

Wk.	Lord's Day	Monday	Tuesday	Wednesday	Thursday	Friday	Saturday
27	☐ 14:22—15:23	☐ 16:1-22	☐ 17:1—18:8	☐ 18:9—19:21	☐ 20:1—21:17	☐ 21:18—22:30	☐ 23:1-25
28	☐ 24:1-22	☐ 25:1-19	☐ 26:1-19	☐ 27:1-26	☐ 28:1-68	☐ 29:1-29	☐ 30:1—31:29
29	☐ 31:30—32:52	☐ 33:1-29	☐ 34:1-12	☐ Josh 1:1-18	☐ 2:1-24	☐ 3:1-17	☐ 4:1-24
30	☐ 5:1-15	☐ 6:1-27	☐ 7:1-26	☐ 8:1-35	☐ 9:1-27	☐ 10:1-43	☐ 11:1—12:24
31	☐ 13:1-33	☐ 14:1—15:63	☐ 16:1—18:28	☐ 19:1-51	☐ 20:1—21:45	☐ 22:1-34	☐ 23:1—24:33
32	☐ Judg 1:1-36	☐ 2:1-23	☐ 3:1-31	☐ 4:1-24	☐ 5:1-31	☐ 6:1-40	☐ 7:1-25
33	☐ 8:1-35	☐ 9:1-57	☐ 10:1—11:40	☐ 12:1—13:25	☐ 14:1—15:20	☐ 16:1-31	☐ 17:1—18:31
34	☐ 19:1-30	☐ 20:1-48	☐ 21:1-25	☐ Ruth 1:1-22	☐ 2:1-23	☐ 3:1-18	☐ 4:1-22
35	☐ 1 Sam 1:1-28	☐ 2:1-36	☐ 3:1—4:22	☐ 5:1—6:21	☐ 7:1—8:22	☐ 9:1-27	☐ 10:1—11:15
36	☐ 12:1—13:23	☐ 14:1-52	☐ 15:1-35	☐ 16:1-23	☐ 17:1-58	☐ 18:1-30	☐ 19:1-24
37	☐ 20:1-42	☐ 21:1—22:23	☐ 23:1—24:22	☐ 25:1-44	☐ 26:1-25	☐ 27:1—28:25	☐ 29:1—30:31
38	☐ 31:1-13	☐ 2 Sam 1:1-27	☐ 2:1-32	☐ 3:1-39	☐ 4:1—5:25	☐ 6:1-23	☐ 7:1-29
39	☐ 8:1—9:13	☐ 10:1—11:27	☐ 12:1-31	☐ 13:1-39	☐ 14:1-33	☐ 15:1—16:23	☐ 17:1—18:33
40	☐ 19:1-43	☐ 20:1—21:22	☐ 22:1-51	☐ 23:1-39	☐ 24:1-25	☐ 1 Kings 1:1-19	☐ 1:20-53
41	☐ 2:1-46	☐ 3:1-28	☐ 4:1-34	☐ 5:1—6:38	☐ 7:1-22	☐ 7:23-51	☐ 8:1-36
42	☐ 8:37-66	☐ 9:1-28	☐ 10:1-29	☐ 11:1-43	☐ 12:1-33	☐ 13:1-34	☐ 14:1-31
43	☐ 15:1-34	☐ 16:1—17:24	☐ 18:1-46	☐ 19:1-21	☐ 20:1-43	☐ 21:1—22:53	☐ 2 Kings 1:1-18
44	☐ 2:1—3:27	☐ 4:1-44	☐ 5:1—6:33	☐ 7:1-20	☐ 8:1-29	☐ 9:1-37	☐ 10:1-36
45	☐ 11:1—12:21	☐ 13:1—14:29	☐ 15:1-38	☐ 16:1-20	☐ 17:1-41	☐ 18:1-37	☐ 19:1-37
46	☐ 20:1—21:26	☐ 22:1-20	☐ 23:1-37	☐ 24:1—25:30	☐ 1 Chron 1:1-54	☐ 2:1—3:24	☐ 4:1—5:26
47	☐ 6:1-81	☐ 7:1-40	☐ 8:1-40	☐ 9:1-44	☐ 10:1—11:47	☐ 12:1-40	☐ 13:1—14:17
48	☐ 15:1—16:43	☐ 17:1-27	☐ 18:1—19:19	☐ 20:1—21:30	☐ 22:1—23:32	☐ 24:1—25:31	☐ 26:1-32
49	☐ 27:1-34	☐ 28:1—29:30	☐ 2 Chron 1:1-17	☐ 2:1—3:17	☐ 4:1—5:14	☐ 6:1-42	☐ 7:1—8:18
50	☐ 9:1—10:19	☐ 11:1—12:16	☐ 13:1—15:19	☐ 16:1—17:19	☐ 18:1—19:11	☐ 20:1-37	☐ 21:1—22:12
51	☐ 23:1—24:27	☐ 25:1—26:23	☐ 27:1—28:27	☐ 29:1-36	☐ 30:1—31:21	☐ 32:1-33	☐ 33:1—34:33
52	☐ 35:1—36:23	☐ Ezra 1:1-11	☐ 2:1-70	☐ 3:1—4:24	☐ 5:1—6:22	☐ 7:1-28	☐ 8:1-36

Reading Schedule for the Recovery Version of the Old Testament with Footnotes

Wk.	Lord's Day	Monday	Tuesday	Wednesday	Thursday	Friday	Saturday
53	9:1—10:44	Neh 1:1-11	2:1—3:32	4:1—5:19	6:1-19	7:1-73	8:1-18
54	9:1-20	9:21-38	10:1—11:36	12:1-47	13:1-31	Esth 1:1-22	2:1—3:15
55	4:1—5:14	6:1—7:10	8:1-17	9:1—10:3	Job 1:1-22	2:1—3:26	4:1—5:27
56	6:1—7:21	8:1—9:35	10:1—11:20	12:1—13:28	14:1—15:35	16:1—17:16	18:1—19:29
57	20:1—21:34	22:1—23:17	24:1—25:6	26:1—27:23	28:1—29:25	30:1—31:40	32:1—33:33
58	34:1—35:16	36:1-33	37:1-24	38:1-41	39:1-30	40:1-24	41:1-34
59	42:1-17	Psa 1:1-6	2:1—3:8	4:1—6:10	7:1—8:9	9:1—10:18	11:1—15:5
60	16:1—17:15	18:1-50	19:1—21:13	22:1-31	23:1—24:10	25:1—27:14	28:1—30:12
61	31:1—32:11	33:1—34:22	35:1—36:12	37:1-40	38:1—39:13	40:1—41:13	42:1—43:5
62	44:1-26	45:1-17	46:1—48:14	49:1—50:23	51:1—52:9	53:1—55:23	56:1—58:11
63	59:1—61:8	62:1—64:10	65:1—67:7	68:1-35	69:1—70:5	71:1—72:20	73:1—74:23
64	75:1—77:20	78:1-72	79:1—81:16	82:1—84:12	85:1—87:7	88:1—89:52	90:1—91:16
65	92:1—94:23	95:1—97:12	98:1—101:8	102:1—103:22	104:1—105:45	106:1-48	107:1-43
66	108:1—109:31	110:1—112:10	113:1—115:18	116:1—118:29	119:1-32	119:33-72	119:73-120
67	119:121-176	120:1—124:8	125:1—128:6	129:1—132:18	133:1—135:21	136:1—138:8	139:1—140:13
68	141:1—144:15	145:1—147:20	148:1—150:6	Prov 1:1-33	2:1—3:35	4:1—5:23	6:1-35
69	7:1—8:36	9:1—10:32	11:1—12:28	13:1—14:35	15:1-33	16:1-33	17:1-28
70	18:1-24	19:1—20:30	21:1—22:29	23:1-35	24:1—25:28	26:1—27:27	28:1—29:27
71	30:1-33	31:1-31	Eccl 1:1-18	2:1—3:22	4:1—5:20	6:1—7:29	8:1—9:18
72	10:1—11:10	12:1-14	S.S 1:1-8	1:9-17	2:1-17	3:1-11	4:1-8
73	4:9-16	5:1-16	6:1-13	7:1-13	8:1-14	Isa 1:1-11	1:12-31
74	2:1-22	3:1-26	4:1-6	5:1-30	6:1-13	7:1-25	8:1-22
75	9:1-21	10:1-34	11:1—12:6	13:1-22	14:1-14	14:15-32	15:1—16:14
76	17:1—18:7	19:1-25	20:1—21:17	22:1-25	23:1-18	24:1-23	25:1-12
77	26:1-21	27:1-13	28:1-29	29:1-24	30:1-33	31:1—32:20	33:1-24
78	34:1-17	35:1-10	36:1-22	37:1-38	38:1—39:8	40:1-31	41:1-29

Reading Schedule for the Recovery Version of the Old Testament with Footnotes

Wk.	Lord's Day	Monday	Tuesday	Wednesday	Thursday	Friday	Saturday
79	☐ 42:1-25	☐ 43:1-28	☐ 44:1-28	☐ 45:1-25	☐ 46:1-13	☐ 47:1-15	☐ 48:1-22
80	☐ 49:1-13	☐ 49:14-26	☐ 50:1—51:23	☐ 52:1-15	☐ 53:1-12	☐ 54:1-17	☐ 55:1-13
81	☐ 56:1-12	☐ 57:1-21	☐ 58:1-14	☐ 59:1-21	☐ 60:1-22	☐ 61:1-11	☐ 62:1-12
82	☐ 63:1-19	☐ 64:1-12	☐ 65:1-25	☐ 66:1-24	☐ Jer 1:1-19	☐ 2:1-19	☐ 2:20-37
83	☐ 3:1-25	☐ 4:1-31	☐ 5:1-31	☐ 6:1-30	☐ 7:1-34	☐ 8:1-22	☐ 9:1-26
84	☐ 10:1-25	☐ 11:1—12:17	☐ 13:1-27	☐ 14:1-22	☐ 15:1-21	☐ 16:1—17:27	☐ 18:1-23
85	☐ 19:1—20:18	☐ 21:1—22:30	☐ 23:1-40	☐ 24:1—25:38	☐ 26:1—27:22	☐ 28:1—29:32	☐ 30:1-24
86	☐ 31:1-23	☐ 31:24-40	☐ 32:1-44	☐ 33:1-26	☐ 34:1-22	☐ 35:1-19	☐ 36:1-32
87	☐ 37:1-21	☐ 38:1-28	☐ 39:1—40:16	☐ 41:1—42:22	☐ 43:1—44:30	☐ 45:1—46:28	☐ 47:1—48:16
88	☐ 48:17-47	☐ 49:1-22	☐ 49:23-39	☐ 50:1-27	☐ 50:28-46	☐ 51:1-27	☐ 51:28-64
89	☐ 52:1-34	☐ Lam 1:1-22	☐ 2:1-22	☐ 3:1-39	☐ 3:40-66	☐ 4:1-22	☐ 5:1-22
90	☐ Ezek 1:1-14	☐ 1:15-28	☐ 2:1—3:27	☐ 4:1—5:17	☐ 6:1—7:27	☐ 8:1—9:11	☐ 10:1—11:25
91	☐ 12:1—13:23	☐ 14:1—15:8	☐ 16:1-63	☐ 17:1—18:32	☐ 19:1-14	☐ 20:1-49	☐ 21:1-32
92	☐ 22:1-31	☐ 23:1-49	☐ 24:1-27	☐ 25:1—26:21	☐ 27:1-36	☐ 28:1-26	☐ 29:1—30:26
93	☐ 31:1—32:32	☐ 33:1-33	☐ 34:1-31	☐ 35:1—36:21	☐ 36:22-38	☐ 37:1-28	☐ 38:1—39:29
94	☐ 40:1-27	☐ 40:28-49	☐ 41:1-26	☐ 42:1—43:27	☐ 44:1-31	☐ 45:1-25	☐ 46:1-24
95	☐ 47:1-23	☐ 48:1-35	☐ Dan 1:1-21	☐ 2:1-30	☐ 2:31-49	☐ 3:1-30	☐ 4:1-37
96	☐ 5:1-31	☐ 6:1-28	☐ 7:1-12	☐ 7:13-28	☐ 8:1-27	☐ 9:1-27	☐ 10:1-21
97	☐ 11:1-22	☐ 11:23-45	☐ 12:1-13	☐ Hosea 1:1-11	☐ 2:1-23	☐ 3:1—4:19	☐ 5:1-15
98	☐ 6:1-11	☐ 7:1-16	☐ 8:1-14	☐ 9:1-17	☐ 10:1-15	☐ 11:1-12	☐ 12:1-14
99	☐ 13:1—14:9	☐ Joel 1:1-20	☐ 2:1-16	☐ 2:17-32	☐ 3:1-21	☐ Amos 1:1-15	☐ 2:1-16
100	☐ 3:1-15	☐ 4:1—5:27	☐ 6:1—7:17	☐ 8:1—9:15	☐ Obad 1-21	☐ Jonah 1:1-17	☐ 2:1—4:11
101	☐ Micah 1:1-16	☐ 2:1—3:12	☐ 4:1—5:15	☐ 6:1—7:20	☐ Nahum 1:1-15	☐ 2:1—3:19	☐ Hab 1:1-17
102	☐ 2:1-20	☐ 3:1-19	☐ Zeph 1:1-18	☐ 2:1-15	☐ 3:1-20	☐ Hag 1:1-15	☐ 2:1-23
103	☐ Zech 1:1-21	☐ 2:1-13	☐ 3:1-10	☐ 4:1-14	☐ 5:1—6:15	☐ 7:1—8:23	☐ 9:1-17
104	☐ 10:1—11:17	☐ 12:1—13:9	☐ 14:1-21	☐ Mal 1:1-14	☐ 2:1-17	☐ 3:1-18	☐ 4:1-6

Reading Schedule for the Recovery Version of the New Testament with Footnotes

Wk.	Lord's Day	Monday	Tuesday	Wednesday	Thursday	Friday	Saturday
1	Matt 1:1-2	1:3-7	1:8-17	1:18-25	2:1-23	3:1-6	3:7-17
2	4:1-11	4:12-25	5:1-4	5:5-12	5:13-20	5:21-26	5:27-48
3	6:1-8	6:9-18	6:19-34	7:1-12	7:13-29	8:1-13	8:14-22
4	8:23-34	9:1-13	9:14-17	9:18-34	9:35—10:5	10:6-25	10:26-42
5	11:1-15	11:16-30	12:1-14	12:15-32	12:33-42	12:43—13:2	13:3-12
6	13:13-30	13:31-43	13:44-58	14:1-13	14:14-21	14:22-36	15:1-20
7	15:21-31	15:32-39	16:1-12	16:13-20	16:21-28	17:1-13	17:14-27
8	18:1-14	18:15-22	18:23-35	19:1-15	19:16-30	20:1-16	20:17-34
9	21:1-11	21:12-22	21:23-32	21:33-46	22:1-22	22:23-33	22:34-46
10	23:1-12	23:13-39	24:1-14	24:15-31	24:32-51	25:1-13	25:14-30
11	25:31-46	26:1-16	26:17-35	26:36-46	26:47-64	26:65-75	27:1-26
12	27:27-44	27:45-56	27:57—28:15	28:16-20	Mark 1:1	1:2-6	1:7-13
13	1:14-28	1:29-45	2:1-12	2:13-28	3:1-19	3:20-35	4:1-25
14	4:26-41	5:1-20	5:21-43	6:1-29	6:30-56	7:1-23	7:24-37
15	8:1-26	8:27—9:1	9:2-29	9:30-50	10:1-16	10:17-34	10:35-52
16	11:1-16	11:17-33	12:1-27	12:28-44	13:1-13	13:14-37	14:1-26
17	14:27-52	14:53-72	15:1-15	15:16-47	16:1-8	16:9-20	Luke 1:1-4
18	1:5-25	1:26-46	1:47-56	1:57-80	2:1-8	2:9-20	2:21-39
19	2:40-52	3:1-20	3:21-38	4:1-13	4:14-30	4:31-44	5:1-26
20	5:27—6:16	6:17-38	6:39-49	7:1-17	7:18-23	7:24-35	7:36-50
21	8:1-15	8:16-25	8:26-39	8:40-56	9:1-17	9:18-26	9:27-36
22	9:37-50	9:51-62	10:1-11	10:12-24	10:25-37	10:38-42	11:1-13
23	11:14-26	11:27-36	11:37-54	12:1-12	12:13-21	12:22-34	12:35-48
24	12:49-59	13:1-9	13:10-17	13:18-30	13:31—14:6	14:7-14	14:15-24
25	14:25-35	15:1-10	15:11-21	15:22-32	16:1-13	16:14-22	16:23-31
26	17:1-19	17:20-37	18:1-14	18:15-30	18:31-43	19:1-10	19:11-27

Reading Schedule for the Recovery Version of the New Testament with Footnotes

Wk.	Lord's Day	Monday	Tuesday	Wednesday	Thursday	Friday	Saturday
27	☐ Luke 19:28-48	☐ 20:1-19	☐ 20:20-38	☐ 20:39—21:4	☐ 21:5-27	☐ 21:28-38	☐ 22:1-20
28	☐ 22:21-38	☐ 22:39-54	☐ 22:55-71	☐ 23:1-43	☐ 23:44-56	☐ 24:1-12	☐ 24:13-35
29	☐ 24:36-53	☐ John 1:1-13	☐ 1:14-18	☐ 1:19-34	☐ 1:35-51	☐ 2:1-11	☐ 2:12-22
30	☐ 2:23—3:13	☐ 3:14-21	☐ 3:22-36	☐ 4:1-14	☐ 4:15-26	☐ 4:27-42	☐ 4:43-54
31	☐ 5:1-16	☐ 5:17-30	☐ 5:31-47	☐ 6:1-15	☐ 6:16-31	☐ 6:32-51	☐ 6:52-71
32	☐ 7:1-9	☐ 7:10-24	☐ 7:25-36	☐ 7:37-52	☐ 7:53—8:11	☐ 8:12-27	☐ 8:28-44
33	☐ 8:45-59	☐ 9:1-13	☐ 9:14-34	☐ 9:35—10:9	☐ 10:10-30	☐ 10:31—11:4	☐ 11:5-22
34	☐ 11:23-40	☐ 11:41-57	☐ 12:1-11	☐ 12:12-24	☐ 12:25-36	☐ 12:37-50	☐ 13:1-11
35	☐ 13:12-30	☐ 13:31-38	☐ 14:1-6	☐ 14:7-20	☐ 14:21-31	☐ 15:1-11	☐ 15:12-27
36	☐ 16:1-15	☐ 16:16-33	☐ 17:1-5	☐ 17:6-13	☐ 17:14-24	☐ 17:25—18:11	☐ 18:12-27
37	☐ 18:28-40	☐ 19:1-16	☐ 19:17-30	☐ 19:31-42	☐ 20:1-13	☐ 20:14-18	☐ 20:19-22
38	☐ 20:23-31	☐ 21:1-14	☐ 21:15-22	☐ 21:23-25	☐ Acts 1:1-8	☐ 1:9-14	☐ 1:15-26
39	☐ 2:1-13	☐ 2:14-21	☐ 2:22-36	☐ 2:37-41	☐ 2:42-47	☐ 3:1-18	☐ 3:19—4:22
40	☐ 4:23-37	☐ 5:1-16	☐ 5:17-32	☐ 5:33-42	☐ 6:1—7:1	☐ 7:2-29	☐ 7:30-60
41	☐ 8:1-13	☐ 8:14-25	☐ 8:26-40	☐ 9:1-19	☐ 9:20-43	☐ 10:1-16	☐ 10:17-33
42	☐ 10:34-48	☐ 11:1-18	☐ 11:19-30	☐ 12:1-25	☐ 13:1-12	☐ 13:13-43	☐ 13:44—14:5
43	☐ 14:6-28	☐ 15:1-12	☐ 15:13-34	☐ 15:35—16:5	☐ 16:6-18	☐ 16:19-40	☐ 17:1-18
44	☐ 17:19-34	☐ 18:1-17	☐ 18:18-28	☐ 19:1-20	☐ 19:21-41	☐ 20:1-12	☐ 20:13-38
45	☐ 21:1-14	☐ 21:15-26	☐ 21:27-40	☐ 22:1-21	☐ 22:22-29	☐ 22:30—23:11	☐ 23:12-15
46	☐ 23:16-30	☐ 23:31—24:21	☐ 24:22—25:5	☐ 25:6-27	☐ 26:1-13	☐ 26:14-32	☐ 27:1-26
47	☐ 27:27—28:10	☐ 28:11-22	☐ 28:23-31	☐ Rom 1:1-2	☐ 1:3-7	☐ 1:8-17	☐ 1:18-25
48	☐ 1:26—2:10	☐ 2:11-29	☐ 3:1-20	☐ 3:21-31	☐ 4:1-12	☐ 4:13-25	☐ 5:1-11
49	☐ 5:12-17	☐ 5:18—6:5	☐ 6:6-11	☐ 6:12-23	☐ 7:1-12	☐ 7:13-25	☐ 8:1-2
50	☐ 8:3-6	☐ 8:7-13	☐ 8:14-25	☐ 8:26-39	☐ 9:1-18	☐ 9:19—10:3	☐ 10:4-15
51	☐ 10:16—11:10	☐ 11:11-22	☐ 11:23-36	☐ 12:1-3	☐ 12:4-21	☐ 13:1-14	☐ 14:1-12
52	☐ 14:13-23	☐ 15:1-13	☐ 15:14-33	☐ 16:1-5	☐ 16:6-24	☐ 16:25-27	☐ 1 Cor 1:1-4

Reading Schedule for the Recovery Version of the New Testament with Footnotes

Wk.	Lord's Day	Monday	Tuesday	Wednesday	Thursday	Friday	Saturday
53	1 Cor 1:5-9 ☐	1:10-17 ☐	1:18-31 ☐	2:1-5 ☐	2:6-10 ☐	2:11-16 ☐	3:1-9 ☐
54	3:10-13 ☐	3:14-23 ☐	4:1-9 ☐	4:10-21 ☐	5:1-13 ☐	6:1-11 ☐	6:12-20 ☐
55	7:1-16 ☐	7:17-24 ☐	7:25-40 ☐	8:1-13 ☐	9:1-15 ☐	9:16-27 ☐	10:1-4 ☐
56	10:5-13 ☐	10:14-33 ☐	11:1-6 ☐	11:7-16 ☐	11:17-26 ☐	11:27-34 ☐	12:1-11 ☐
57	12:12-22 ☐	12:23-31 ☐	13:1-13 ☐	14:1-12 ☐	14:13-25 ☐	14:26-33 ☐	14:34-40 ☐
58	15:1-19 ☐	15:20-28 ☐	15:29-34 ☐	15:35-49 ☐	15:50-58 ☐	16:1-9 ☐	16:10-24 ☐
59	2 Cor 1:1-4 ☐	1:5-14 ☐	1:15-22 ☐	1:23—2:11 ☐	2:12-17 ☐	3:1-6 ☐	3:7-11 ☐
60	3:12-18 ☐	4:1-6 ☐	4:7-12 ☐	4:13-18 ☐	5:1-8 ☐	5:9-15 ☐	5:16-21 ☐
61	6:1-13 ☐	6:14—7:4 ☐	7:5-16 ☐	8:1-15 ☐	8:16-24 ☐	9:1-15 ☐	10:1-6 ☐
62	10:7-18 ☐	11:1-15 ☐	11:16-33 ☐	12:1-10 ☐	12:11-21 ☐	13:1-10 ☐	13:11-14 ☐
63	Gal 1:1-5 ☐	1:6-14 ☐	1:15-24 ☐	2:1-13 ☐	2:14-21 ☐	3:1-4 ☐	3:5-14 ☐
64	3:15-22 ☐	3:23-29 ☐	4:1-7 ☐	4:8-20 ☐	4:21-31 ☐	5:1-12 ☐	5:13-21 ☐
65	5:22-26 ☐	6:1-10 ☐	6:11-15 ☐	6:16-18 ☐	Eph 1:1-3 ☐	1:4-6 ☐	1:7-10 ☐
66	1:11-14 ☐	1:15-18 ☐	1:19-23 ☐	2:1-5 ☐	2:6-10 ☐	2:11-14 ☐	2:15-18 ☐
67	2:19-22 ☐	3:1-7 ☐	3:8-13 ☐	3:14-18 ☐	3:19-21 ☐	4:1-4 ☐	4:5-10 ☐
68	4:11-16 ☐	4:17-24 ☐	4:25-32 ☐	5:1-10 ☐	5:11-21 ☐	5:22-26 ☐	5:27-33 ☐
69	6:1-9 ☐	6:10-14 ☐	6:15-18 ☐	6:19-24 ☐	Phil 1:1-7 ☐	1:8-18 ☐	1:19-26 ☐
70	1:27—2:4 ☐	2:5-11 ☐	2:12-16 ☐	2:17-30 ☐	3:1-6 ☐	3:7-11 ☐	3:12-16 ☐
71	3:17-21 ☐	4:1-9 ☐	4:10-23 ☐	Col 1:1-8 ☐	1:9-13 ☐	1:14-23 ☐	1:24-29 ☐
72	2:1-7 ☐	2:8-15 ☐	2:16-23 ☐	3:1-4 ☐	3:5-15 ☐	3:16-25 ☐	4:1-18 ☐
73	1 Thes 1:1-3 ☐	1:4-10 ☐	2:1-12 ☐	2:13—3:5 ☐	3:6-13 ☐	4:1-10 ☐	4:11—5:11 ☐
74	5:12-28 ☐	2 Thes 1:1-12 ☐	2:1-17 ☐	3:1-18 ☐	1 Tim 1:1-2 ☐	1:3-4 ☐	1:5-14 ☐
75	1:15-20 ☐	2:1-7 ☐	2:8-15 ☐	3:1-13 ☐	3:14—4:5 ☐	4:6-16 ☐	5:1-25 ☐
76	6:1-10 ☐	6:11-21 ☐	2 Tim 1:1-10 ☐	1:11-18 ☐	2:1-15 ☐	2:16-26 ☐	3:1-13 ☐
77	3:14—4:8 ☐	4:9-22 ☐	Titus 1:1-4 ☐	1:5-16 ☐	2:1-15 ☐	3:1-8 ☐	3:9-15 ☐
78	Philem 1:1-11 ☐	1:12-25 ☐	Heb 1:1-2 ☐	1:3-5 ☐	1:6-14 ☐	2:1-9 ☐	2:10-18 ☐

Reading Schedule for the Recovery Version of the New Testament with Footnotes

Wk.	Lord's Day	Monday	Tuesday	Wednesday	Thursday	Friday	Saturday
79	☐ Heb 3:1-6	☐ 3:7-19	☐ 4:1-9	☐ 4:10-13	☐ 4:14-16	☐ 5:1-10	☐ 5:11—6:3
80	☐ 6:4-8	☐ 6:9-20	☐ 7:1-10	☐ 7:11-28	☐ 8:1-6	☐ 8:7-13	☐ 9:1-4
81	☐ 9:5-14	☐ 9:15-28	☐ 10:1-18	☐ 10:19-28	☐ 10:29-39	☐ 11:1-6	☐ 11:7-19
82	☐ 11:20-31	☐ 11:32-40	☐ 12:1-2	☐ 12:3-13	☐ 12:14-17	☐ 12:18-26	☐ 12:27-29
83	☐ 13:1-7	☐ 13:8-12	☐ 13:13-15	☐ 13:16-25	☐ James 1:1-8	☐ 1:9-18	☐ 1:19-27
84	☐ 2:1-13	☐ 2:14-26	☐ 3:1-18	☐ 4:1-10	☐ 4:11-17	☐ 5:1-12	☐ 5:13-20
85	☐ 1 Pet 1:1-2	☐ 1:3-4	☐ 1:5	☐ 1:6-9	☐ 1:10-12	☐ 1:13-17	☐ 1:18-25
86	☐ 2:1-3	☐ 2:4-8	☐ 2:9-17	☐ 2:18-25	☐ 3:1-13	☐ 3:14-22	☐ 4:1-6
87	☐ 4:7-16	☐ 4:17-19	☐ 5:1-4	☐ 5:5-9	☐ 5:10-14	☐ 2 Pet 1:1-2	☐ 1:3-4
88	☐ 1:5-8	☐ 1:9-11	☐ 1:12-18	☐ 1:19-21	☐ 2:1-3	☐ 2:4-11	☐ 2:12-22
89	☐ 3:1-6	☐ 3:7-9	☐ 3:10-12	☐ 3:13-15	☐ 3:16	☐ 3:17-18	☐ 1 John 1:1-2
90	☐ 1:3-4	☐ 1:5	☐ 1:6	☐ 1:7	☐ 1:8-10	☐ 2:1-2	☐ 2:3-11
91	☐ 2:12-14	☐ 2:15-19	☐ 2:20-23	☐ 2:24-27	☐ 2:28-29	☐ 3:1-5	☐ 3:6-10
92	☐ 3:11-18	☐ 3:19-24	☐ 4:1-6	☐ 4:7-11	☐ 4:12-15	☐ 4:16—5:3	☐ 5:4-13
93	☐ 5:14-17	☐ 5:18-21	☐ 2 John 1:1-3	☐ 1:4-9	☐ 1:10-13	☐ 3 John 1:1-6	☐ 1:7-14
94	☐ Jude 1:1-4	☐ 1:5-10	☐ 1:11-19	☐ 1:20-25	☐ Rev 1:1-3	☐ 1:4-6	☐ 1:7-11
95	☐ 1:12-13	☐ 1:14-16	☐ 1:17-20	☐ 2:1-6	☐ 2:7	☐ 2:8-9	☐ 2:10-11
96	☐ 2:12-14	☐ 2:15-17	☐ 2:18-23	☐ 2:24-29	☐ 3:1-3	☐ 3:4-6	☐ 3:7-9
97	☐ 3:10-13	☐ 3:14-18	☐ 3:19-22	☐ 4:1-5	☐ 4:6-7	☐ 4:8-11	☐ 5:1-6
98	☐ 5:7-14	☐ 6:1-8	☐ 6:9-17	☐ 7:1-8	☐ 7:9-17	☐ 8:1-6	☐ 8:7-12
99	☐ 8:13—9:11	☐ 9:12-21	☐ 10:1-4	☐ 10:5-11	☐ 11:1-4	☐ 11:5-14	☐ 11:15-19
100	☐ 12:1-4	☐ 12:5-9	☐ 12:10-18	☐ 13:1-10	☐ 13:11-18	☐ 14:1-5	☐ 14:6-12
101	☐ 14:13-20	☐ 15:1-8	☐ 16:1-12	☐ 16:13-21	☐ 17:1-6	☐ 17:7-18	☐ 18:1-8
102	☐ 18:9—19:4	☐ 19:5-10	☐ 19:11-16	☐ 19:17-21	☐ 20:1-6	☐ 20:7-10	☐ 20:11-15
103	☐ 21:1	☐ 21:2	☐ 21:3-8	☐ 21:9-13	☐ 21:14-18	☐ 21:19-21	☐ 21:22-27
104	☐ 22:1	☐ 22:2	☐ 22:3-11	☐ 22:12-15	☐ 22:16-17	☐ 22:18-21	

Week 1 — Day 1   Today's verses

2 Tim. Be diligent to present yourself approved
2:15 to God, an unashamed workman, cutting
straight the word of the truth.
3:16 All Scripture is God-breathed and profitable for teaching, for conviction, for cor-
rection, for instruction in righteousness.

_____
Date

Week 1 — Day 2   Today's verses

John ...For this I have been born, and for this
18:37 I have come into the world, that I would
testify to the truth. Everyone who is of the
truth hears My voice.
3 John For I rejoiced greatly at the brothers' com-
3-4 ing and testifying to your *steadfastness
in the* truth, even as you walk in truth.
I have no greater joy than these things,
that I hear that my children are walking
in the truth.

_____
Date

Week 1 — Day 3   Today's verses

John Jesus said to him, I am the way and the
14:6 reality and the life; no one comes to the
Father except through Me.
Rom. And if the Spirit of the One who raised
8:11 Jesus from the dead dwells in you, He
who raised Christ from the dead will also
give life to your mortal bodies through His
Spirit who indwells you.

_____
Date

Week 1 — Day 4   Today's verses

1 Tim. But if I delay, *I write* that you may know
3:15-16 how one ought to conduct himself in
the house of God, which is the church
of the living God, the pillar and base of
the truth. And confessedly, great is the
mystery of godliness: He who was manifested in the flesh, justified in the Spirit,
seen by angels, preached among the
nations, believed on in the world, taken
up in glory.

_____
Date

Week 1 — Day 5   Today's verses

Eph. And He subjected all things under His
1:22-23 feet and gave Him *to be* Head over all
things to the church, which is His Body,
the fullness of the One who fills all in all.
6:15 And having shod your feet with the firm
foundation of the gospel of peace.

_____
Date

Week 1 — Day 6   Today's verses

1 Tim. This is good and acceptable in the sight of
2:3-4 our Savior God, who desires all men to be
saved and to come to the full knowledge
of the truth.
Col. Because of the hope laid up for you in the
1:5 heavens, of which you heard before in
the word of the truth of the gospel.

_____
Date

Week 2 — Day 4   Today's verses

John
17:19-21

And for their sake I sanctify Myself, that they themselves also may be sanctified in truth. And I do not ask concerning these only; but concerning those also who believe into Me through their word, that they all may be one; even as You, Father, are in Me and I in You, that they also may be in Us; that the world may believe that You have sent Me.

Eph.
5:26

That He might sanctify her, cleansing *her* by the washing of the water in the word.

_____
Date

Week 2 — Day 5   Today's verses

John
17:24

Father, *concerning* that which You have given Me, I desire that they also may be with Me where I am, that they may behold My glory, which You have given Me, for You loved Me before the foundation of the world.

Eph.
4:16

Out from whom all the Body...causes the growth of the Body unto the building up of itself in love.

_____
Date

Week 2 — Day 6   Today's verses

John
17:21-23

That they all may be one; even as You, Father, are in Me and I in You, that they also may be in Us; that the world may believe that You have sent Me. And the glory which You have given Me I have given to them, that they may be one, even as We are one; I in them, and You in Me, that they may be perfected into one, that the world may know that You have sent Me and have loved them even as You have loved Me.

_____
Date

Week 2 — Day 1   Today's verses

John
8:12

...Jesus spoke to them, saying, I am the light of the world; he who follows Me shall by no means walk in darkness, but shall have the light of life.

Eph.
1:17-18

That the God of our Lord Jesus Christ, the Father of glory, may give to you a spirit of wisdom and revelation in the full knowledge of Him, the eyes of your heart having been enlightened, that you may know...

_____
Date

Week 2 — Day 2   Today's verses

John
8:32

And you shall know the truth, and the truth shall set you free.

36

If therefore the Son sets you free, you shall be free indeed.

17:17

Sanctify them in the truth; Your word is truth.

_____
Date

Week 2 — Day 3   Today's verses

John
16:13

But when He, the Spirit of reality, comes, He will guide you into all the reality; for He will not speak from Himself, but what He hears He will speak; and He will declare to you the things that are coming.

1 John
5:6

...The Spirit is the reality.

_____
Date

Week 3 — Day 4 Today's verses

John 16:13-14 But when He, the Spirit of reality, comes, He will guide you into all the reality; for He will not speak from Himself, but what He hears He will speak; and He will declare to you the things that are coming. He will glorify Me, for He will receive of Mine and will declare *it* to you.

Date

Week 3 — Day 5 Today's verses

1 John 5:6 This is He who came through water and blood, Jesus Christ; not in the water only, but in the water and in the blood; and the Spirit is He who testifies, because the Spirit is the reality.

20 And we know that the Son of God has come and has given us an understanding that we might know Him who is true; and we are in Him who is true, in His Son Jesus Christ. This is the true God and eternal life.

Date

Week 3 — Day 6 Today's verses

John 17:3 And this is eternal life, that they may know You, the only true God, and Him whom You have sent, Jesus Christ.

14:6 Jesus said to him, I am the way and the reality and the life; no one comes to the Father except through Me.

1 John 5:20 …This is the true God and eternal life.

Date

Week 3 — Day 1 Today's verses

John 1:14 And the Word became flesh and tabernacled among us (and we beheld His glory, glory as of the only Begotten from the Father), full of grace and reality.

1 John 5:6 This is He who came through water and blood, Jesus Christ; not in the water only, but in the water and in the blood; and the Spirit is He who testifies, because the Spirit is the reality.

Date

Week 3 — Day 2 Today's verses

Eph. 1:13 In whom you also, having heard the word of the truth, the gospel of your salvation, in Him also believing, you were sealed with the Holy Spirit of the promise.

Col. 1:5 Because of the hope laid up for you in the heavens, of which you heard before in the word of the truth of the gospel.

John 17:17 Sanctify them in the truth; Your word is truth.

Date

Week 3 — Day 3 Today's verses

Eccl. 1:2 Vanity of vanities, says the Preacher; vanity of vanities; all is vanity.

1 John 5:20-21 And we know that the Son of God has come and has given us an understanding that we might know Him who is true; and we are in Him who is true, in His Son Jesus Christ. This is the true God and eternal life. Little children, guard yourselves from idols.

Date

Week 4 — Day 4   Today's verses

Matt. ...Jesus cried out again with a loud voice
27:50-51 and yielded up His spirit. And behold, the
          veil of the temple was split in two from
          top to bottom...
Heb.   Having therefore, brothers, boldness for
10:19-20 entering the *Holy of* Holies in the blood of
          Jesus, which *entrance* He initiated for us
          as a new and living way through the veil,
          that is, His flesh.

_____
Date

Week 4 — Day 5   Today's verses

Rev.   And on this side and on that side of the
22:2   river was the tree of life, producing twelve
       fruits, yielding its fruit each month; and
       the leaves of the tree are for the healing of
       the nations.
1 Cor. But he who is joined to the Lord is one
6:17   spirit.

_____
Date

Week 4 — Day 6   Today's verses

John   Abide in Me and I in you. As the branch
15:4   cannot bear fruit of itself unless it abides
       in the vine, so neither *can* you unless you
       abide in Me.
Gal.   I am crucified with Christ; and *it is* no lon-
2:20   ger I *who* live, but *it is* Christ *who* lives in
       me; and the *life* which I now live in the
       flesh I live in faith, the *faith* of the Son of
       God, who loved me and gave Himself up
       for me.

_____
Date

Week 4 — Day 1   Today's verses

Gen.   And God said, Let Us make man in Our
1:26   image, according to Our likeness; and let
       them have dominion...over all the
       earth...
2:9   ...Out of the ground Jehovah God caused
       to grow every tree that is pleasant to the
       sight and good for food, as well as the tree
       of life in the middle of the garden and the
       tree of the knowledge of good and evil.

_____
Date

Week 4 — Day 2   Today's verses

John   I am the vine; you are the branches. He
15:5   who abides in Me and I in him, he bears
       much fruit; for apart from Me you can do
       nothing.
1:4   In Him was life, and the life was the light
       of men.

_____
Date

Week 4 — Day 3   Today's verses

Rev.   He who has an ear, let him hear what the
2:7   Spirit says to the churches. To him who
       overcomes, to him I will give to eat of the
       tree of life, which is in the Paradise of
       God.
22:14 Blessed are those who wash their robes
       that they may have right to the tree of life
       and may enter by the gates into the city.

_____
Date

Week 6 — Day 4 Today's verses

Matt. And behold, a voice out of the heavens,
3:17 saying, This is My Son, the Beloved, in
 whom I have found My delight.

John But as many as received Him, to them He
1:12-13 gave the authority to become children of
 God, to those who believe into His name,
 who were begotten not of blood, nor of
 the will of the flesh, nor of the will of man,
 but of God.

_____
Date

Week 6 — Day 5 Today's verses

Rev. And made us a kingdom, priests to His
1:6 God and Father, to Him be the glory and
 the might forever and ever. Amen.

Gal. …Those who practice such things will not
5:21, 25 inherit the kingdom of God….If we live
 by the Spirit, let us also walk by the Spirit.

_____
Date

Week 6 — Day 6 Today's verses

2 Pet. For in this way the entrance into the eter-
1:11 nal kingdom of our Lord and Savior Jesus
 Christ will be richly and bountifully supplied to you.

Matt. Your kingdom come; Your will be done,
6:10 as in heaven, so also on earth.

_____
Date

Week 6 — Day 1 Today's verses

Eph. So then you are no longer strangers and
2:19 sojourners, but you are fellow citizens
 with the saints and members of the household of God.

1 Thes. So that you might walk in a manner wor-
2:12 thy of God, who calls you into His own
 kingdom and glory.

_____
Date

Week 6 — Day 2 Today's verses

John Jesus answered, Truly, truly, I say to you,
3:5 Unless one is born of water and the Spirit,
 he cannot enter into the kingdom of God.

Rom. For the kingdom of God is not eating and
14:17 drinking, but righteousness and peace
 and joy in the Holy Spirit.

_____
Date

Week 6 — Day 3 Today's verses

Matt. Truly I say to you, Whatever you bind on
18:18 the earth shall have been bound in
 heaven, and whatever you loose on the
 earth shall have been loosed in heaven.

Col. Who delivered us out of the authority of
1:13 darkness and transferred us into the kingdom of the Son of His love.

_____
Date

Week 7 — Day 1 Today's verses

Matt. 16:16-18 And Simon Peter answered and said, You are the Christ, the Son of the living God. And Jesus answered and said to him, Blessed are you, Simon Barjona, because flesh and blood has not revealed *this* to you, but My Father who is in the heavens. And I also say to you that you are Peter, and upon this rock I will build My church, and the gates of Hades shall not prevail against it.

Date _____

Week 7 — Day 2 Today's verses

Matt. 16:19 I will give to you the keys of the kingdom of the heavens, and whatever you bind on the earth shall have been bound in the heavens, and whatever you loose on the earth shall have been loosed in the heavens.

21 From that time Jesus began to show to His disciples that He must go to Jerusalem and suffer many things from the elders and chief priests and scribes and be killed and on the third day be raised.

Date _____

Week 7 — Day 3 Today's verses

Matt. 16:23-24 But He turned and said to Peter, Get behind Me, Satan! You are a stumbling block to Me, for you are not setting your mind on the things of God, but on the things of men. Then Jesus said to His disciples, If anyone wants to come after Me, let him deny himself and take up his cross and follow Me.

Date _____

Week 7 — Day 4 Today's verses

Matt. 7:21-23 Not everyone who says to Me, Lord, Lord, will enter into the kingdom of the heavens, but he who does the will of My Father who is in the heavens. Many will say to Me in that day, Lord, Lord, *was it* not in Your name *that* we prophesied, and in Your name cast out demons, and in Your name did many works of power? And then I will declare to them: I never knew you. Depart from Me, you workers of lawlessness.

Date _____

Week 7 — Day 5 Today's verses

Matt. 16:24 Then Jesus said to His disciples, If anyone wants to come after Me, let him...take up his cross and follow Me.

Phil. 3:10 To know Him and the power of His resurrection and the fellowship of His sufferings, being conformed to His death.

Date _____

Week 7 — Day 6 Today's verses

Matt. 16:25-26 For whoever wants to save his soul-life shall lose it; but whoever loses his soul-life for My sake shall find it. For what shall a man be profited if he gains the whole world, but forfeits his soul-life? Or what shall a man give in exchange for his soul-life?

Luke 9:25 For what is a man profited if he gains the whole world but loses or forfeits himself?

Date _____

Week 8 — Day 1

Today's verses

John 1:29 ...Behold, the Lamb of God, who takes away the sin of the world!

Heb. 9:22 And almost all things are purified by blood according to the law, and without shedding of blood there is no forgiveness.

John 19:34 But one of the soldiers pierced His side with a spear, and immediately there came out blood and water.

Date _____

Week 8 — Day 2

Today's verses

Eph. 4:18 Being darkened in their understanding, alienated from the life of God...

Rev. 22:1-2 And he showed me a river of water of life, bright as crystal, proceeding out of the throne of God and of the Lamb in the middle of its street. And on this side and on that side of the river was the tree of life...

Date _____

Week 8 — Day 3

Today's verses

Gen. 2:21-23 And Jehovah God caused a deep sleep to fall upon the man, and he slept; and He took one of his ribs and closed up the flesh in its place. And Jehovah God built the rib, which He had taken from the man, into a woman and brought her to the man. And the man said, This time this is bone of my bones and flesh of my flesh; this one shall be called Woman because this one was taken out of Man.

Date _____

Week 8 — Day 4

Today's verses

Num. 9:12 They shall not leave any of it until the morning, nor break a bone of it...

John 19:36 For these things happened that the Scripture might be fulfilled: "No bone of His shall be broken."

Heb. 7:16 Who has been appointed not according to the law of a fleshy commandment but according to the power of an indestructible life.

Date _____

Week 8 — Day 5

Today's verses

Eph. 5:25-27 Husbands, love your wives even as Christ also loved the church and gave Himself up for her that He might sanctify her, cleansing *her* by the washing of the water in the word, that He might present the church to Himself glorious, not having spot or wrinkle or any such things, but that she would be holy and without blemish.

Date _____

Week 8 — Day 6

Today's verses

Eph. 5:29-30 For no one ever hated his own flesh, but nourishes and cherishes it, even as Christ also the church, because we are members of His Body.

32 This mystery is great, but I speak with regard to Christ and the church.

Rev. 21:2 And I saw the holy city, New Jerusalem, coming down out of heaven from God, prepared as a bride adorned for her husband.

Date _____

Week 9 — Day 4   Today's verses

Rom. ...The gospel of God...concerning His Son,
1:1, 3-4 who came out of the seed of David according to the flesh, who was designated the Son of God in power according to the Spirit of holiness out of the resurrection of the dead, Jesus Christ our Lord.

Heb. For it was fitting for Him, for whom are all
2:10 things and through whom are all things, in leading many sons into glory...

Date

Week 9 — Day 5   Today's verses

Rom. But if Christ is in you, though the body is
8:10-11 dead because of sin, the spirit is life because of righteousness. And if the Spirit of the One who raised Jesus from the dead dwells in you, He who raised Christ from the dead will also give life to your mortal bodies through His Spirit who indwells you.

Date

Week 9 — Day 6   Today's verses

Rom. For the law of the Spirit of life has freed me
8:2 in Christ Jesus from the law of sin and of death.

29 Because those whom He foreknew, He also predestinated *to be* conformed to the image of His Son, that He might be the Firstborn among many brothers.

Date

Week 9 — Day 1   Today's verses

Gal. To them we yielded with the subjection
2:5 *demanded* not even for an hour, that the truth of the gospel might remain with you.

16 And knowing that a man is not justified out of works of law, but through faith in Jesus Christ...

1 Cor. But of Him you are in Christ Jesus, who
1:30 became wisdom to us from God: both righteousness and sanctification and redemption.

Date

Week 9 — Day 2   Today's verses

Rom. Now to Him who is able to establish you
16:25 according to my gospel, that is, the proclamation of Jesus Christ, according to the revelation of the mystery, which has been kept in silence in the times of the ages.

Gal. He therefore who bountifully supplies to
3:5 you the Spirit and does works of power among you, *does He do it* out of the works of law or out of the hearing of faith?

Date

Week 9 — Day 3   Today's verses

Rom. For I am not ashamed of the gospel, for it
1:16-17 is the power of God unto salvation to everyone who believes, both to Jew first and to Greek. For the righteousness of God is revealed in it out of faith to faith, as it is written, "But the righteous shall have life and live by faith."

Date